This book is dedicated to my longtime client and friend,
Robert "Bob" Carpenter, 1928-2015, who taught me the
importance of dealing with clients in person.

Property Management
A-Z

K. RICHARDS

Cover Design: David Ellenwood
Illustrations: David Ellenwood
Editor: Tanya Wlodarczyk
Interior Design: Tanya Wlodarczyk

Website: www.PortolaRentals.com
Facebook: www.facebook.com/PortolaPropertyManagement
Email: kathleen@portolarentals.com
Printed in the United States of America

Property
Management
A-Z

K. RICHARDS

Acknowledgements

I want to first thank Dan Heiser, my retired fireman, for always having dinner on the table when I get home from work and for doing the Costco office supply run for us ladies. Thanks for making me laugh all these years. I am truly blessed.

To my Team, which includes my staff and vendors, for making me look good and providing the excellent customer service my clients have come to expect from us. Portola Property Management, Inc. and Kathleen Richards wouldn't be where we are today without all of your efforts and support. A true Team! I am blessed.

To all my past and current property owners, tenants, my students, and the crazies, over the years you have all made me a better property manager. I have learned something from all of you. I am blessed.

And last but not least, I want to acknowledge all of my colleagues, friends, mentors, and students that have requested and encouraged me to write a book on property management. It has been a goal of mine since 2009 but I could never get it off the ground. I have to thank my editor and expert guide to the publishing process Tanya Wlodarczyk. She helped me turn my dream and ideas into something tangible. I am blessed.

Table of Contents

Index

Introduction

This book is a culmination of my weekly blog, which started in 2009, my teaching workshops at Cabrillo College, my participation in NARPM (National Association of Residential Property Managers) from local chapter President to state chapter board member, my experience as a court expert witness, and finally my 10+ years as a professional property manager. I hope this book will be used as a quick reference guide for the many facets of property management (we do more than just collect rent!), help you decide if being a landlord is for you, and if not, then how to find a good property manager. But above all I wish you success in your property management business!

So how does one become a property manager? I have yet to meet someone who said, "When I grow up I want to be a property manager." Everyone I meet who loves this business found their way into it by accident. So, how did I get here?

I have always been someone who likes to know how things work. I am super organized and always like to find a better, more efficient way of doing things. I love being hands-on and helping people. As far back as I can remember I wanted to own a business.

So when the question was asked of me, "What do you want to be when you grow up?" At the age of 10 I wanted to be a policewoman (to serve and protect), an auto mechanic (have my own garage with only women as my clientele) or a missionary (I wanted to see the world).

I loved school and learning and as the eldest of 5 to a single mother, I saw going to college as my way out of poverty. I worked to put myself through college and received a BA Degree in International Studies with a minor in Economics from the University of the Pacific in Stockton, CA.

I landed a position in Washington D.C. for a State Department subcontractor as a cross-cultural trainer for foreign government officials. The job was awesome, however, my love was in California so once my contract was up I returned to home. I went on to work in marketing for Microsoft in California when we were a still a small group on Sand Hill Rd, in Menlo Park, CA. At the time Microsoft offered a very good employee benefit that I took advantage of and while working 60 hour work weeks I went back for my master's degree in organizational development, human resources, and management. Thank you Bill Gates and Microsoft.

Soon after receiving my master's, my department at Microsoft was incorporated into Microsoft, Seattle. I took the buyout and decided I would go overseas. I had lived in Sweden and Mexico previously and was soon on my way to Japan to teach English to junior high students. However, with my business background I was able to leverage connections and was soon working nights and weekends leading business and cross-cultural training workshops for Civil Service Government Employees. I loved my three years in Japan and especially enjoyed learning about the culture and traveling all over Asia. For example, in Japan there is a misconception that when people say "yes" to something, it means that they understand you or agree with you. What they are really saying is "Yes I hear you," not "Yes I agree," or "Yes, I will do what you say." Knowing small differences in communication styles helps me speak to clients from their perspective and helps create successful working relationships. Understanding different cultures has been a huge benefit in the property management business since you have to deal with many different cultures in all aspects from owners, tenants and vendors.

Upon returning to the States I taught at San Jose State University for a few years and then returned to the business world where I worked for a hedge fund. During this time I started to buy rental properties for my future retirement and I hired property management companies. I had both good and bad experiences so I started to educate myself about the law, tenant rights, and how to manage rentals as a business. Dan, my man, and I had also remodeled several of our homes and his rentals so I became very comfortable with all the different construction and maintenance aspects of owning real estate.

When Dan retired from the fire department we moved back to Santa Cruz, CA full time. I had spent enough years commuting over the hill to Silicon Valley that I knew I wasn't going to do that drive again, so I decided to get my real estate license and do mortgages. This was in 2004–the peak of the subprime market. With my economics degree and just pure common sense I could see the market was out of whack. The people coming to me wanting to buy a home with no money down and not a penny to their name didn't like it when I told them they couldn't afford it. So they went to someone else that was able to put them into their dream home that two years later turned into their biggest nightmare. I decided it wasn't the right niche for me. I can honestly say I never put anyone into a loan they couldn't afford.

All my friends and accounting professionals kept telling me I should do property management, so I gave it a try. I worked for a local property management company and found that I loved it. I had finally found my calling. I loved the relationships of working with owners, tenants, and vendors. I knew the construction and trade lingo so dealing with vendors was easy. I owned my own rentals so I understood the owner perspective.

I remember saying out loud, "It would be great to buy an established property management company from someone who is retiring." While cruising around Craigslist I decided to see what was happening in Santa Cruz and there it was a business for sale! Three weeks later I had purchased a 20-year-old business from a retiring property manager. Ten years later here I sit.

So that is the story of how I grew up to be a property manager and business owner.

I suspect that the reader of this book has had a similar circuitous route to becoming a property owner and landlord. The information in this book is not intended as legal or accounting advice it is a beginning framework and explanation of what is involved and what you need to know in order to manage real estate as an investment– which is exactly what being a landlord is all about. I hope this book becomes a good starting point for your education and a future reference tool as you learn more about the profession.

A

Accidental Landlord, Accounting, Advertising, Addendums – Rental Agreement/Lease

Accidental Landlord

Many people have had to become accidental landlords since the real estate market crash. What does this mean? Simply stated, a property owner can't sell their home because they owe more on it than its value but they are able to make the mortgage payments. This situation locks people into the home. They can't sell so if they want to relocate for a job opportunity or if they need to move into a larger home due to an expanding family they aren't able to do so. They are stuck and tied to their current home. Sometimes the only option they have is to rent the house out so that is how they end up in the landlording business. Often these people don't know how to be landlords so what options are at their disposal? One is to get educated and do it yourself or two, hire a professional property manager.

Keep in mind that you have a lot of realtors whose livelihood has dried up so they've decided to go into property management. Often they don't have the skills or knowledge to do it and this is when you hear the horror stories from property owners.

So make sure to find a dedicated property manager who will be with you and can be your advisor for the long run.

Accounting

This is probably one of the most important aspects of property management. Even if you have just one property I can't stress the importance of doing proper accounting. You don't have to take a QuickBooks class but you do have to have a system to track all rent payments and deposits, late fees, repairs, paid utilities, advertising, maintenance, property taxes, insurance, etc. Even if you have a simple system in place it will make your accountant happy at the end of the year, but more importantly it will help you understand if you are reaching your investment property goals. The only way you can fully understand the financial implications and know whether it is better to sell the property or keep it as a rental is through accounting and knowing the numbers.

As a professional I use a software program by the name of Appfolio for my business but for my personal rentals I use a simple MS Excel spreadsheet that looks like a check register that adds and subtracts the numbers I put into the columns. It takes me about 2 hours per month to update my spreadsheet and my accountant loves me. In addition, I have a large envelop for each rental that all my receipts for each property go into. At the end of the year I print my rental spreadsheet and staple it to the front of the envelope and hand to my accountant. The back-up receipts are in the envelope in case the CPA needs to see the detail but my summary ledger on the front is usually more than enough. It doesn't matter what system you use just have a system that you will stick with through the year.

Advertising

How do you advertise a vacant property? Do you use Craigslist, word-of-mouth, a "For Rent" sign in the front yard, newspaper ad, all of the previous mentioned? Well, I stopped newspaper advertising years ago. However, it really depends upon your market. In my business I only use online advertising, but that doesn't work for my personal rentals in California's Sierra Foothills. Everyone in the small town still picks up the local newspaper to find a rental. So you have to do some research and see what works in your area.

Generally speaking the Internet is where most people will look for rentals so I will address online advertising briefly. If you do use Craigslist, please put up as many photos as allowed. A word of caution here, please do not put the street name or property address anywhere in your listing including the photos. There are many scammers out there who will copy your ad and redirect people to their version of the advertisement. It's a waste of time to advertise a property with no photos. People will think you're not showing the property because it is either in bad shape or in a bad area. You also want to keep the text short and to the point. I often laugh at how people advertise their property like they are selling it. Here is an example, "Quiet, serene, private executive home for rent. This custom home has three spacious bedrooms with custom paint, crown molding, dual pane windows and hardwood floors. Each bedroom has a large walk-in closet. The kitchen is a chef's delight with professional 6 burner gas stove, and subzero refrigerator." They aren't selling they are renting it. People looking to rent are combing hundreds of ads daily so keep it to the point. Namely, type of property (Single Family Residence, Condo, Apartment, Townhouse) single level or multi-story, number of bedrooms, number of bathrooms, garage, yard, neighborhood, rent price and security deposit price. Then give your email address or contact number. An example of a better ad would look like this, "Seabright neighborhood executive style single level home with 3 bedroom, 3 bath, kitchen complete with all the latest appliances, hardwood floors throughout, 2 car garage, backyard and close to shopping and easy freeway access for commuters." Notice this ad is more direct and to the point and less flowery. Stick to the facts. People can see the photos for more details and let's face it they will see the home before they apply.

Keep in mind it is illegal, according to Fair Housing laws, to use words that could be considered discriminatory. You wouldn't believe it but phrases such as: "family friendly home," "perfect for student or senior," "female only," "master bedroom," or "walk-in closet" are violations of Fair Housing Law. So what if you have a community that caters to seniors over a certain age? Then you would say, "This is a 55 years plus community." Another exception is if you are renting a room in your home or the cottage behind the home you live in. You can then say things like "female only," "prefer mature adult 55 years and older." Fair Housing allows you to be more selective when you are sharing your living space. You can't use words like "walk to beach" because what if someone is in a wheel chair?

I know it sounds ridiculous but I use words like "a stone's throw," "1 block to beach," "executive style home," or "close to college" to appeal to certain people that may want to rent the property. State the facts of the property and you will be ok.

Addendums – Rental Agreement/Lease

So what addendums do you need? My leases are about 40 pages! People gasp when they hear this but the actual lease is only 6 pages; the rest are addendums and instructions for the tenants. I have found that it is better to explain everything that is expected of the resident. Then they are able to follow the rules and there are no problems, especially when it comes time to move out and return the deposit.

Make sure to include the addendums required by law such as the lead addendum and booklet, which is required for all properties built from 1978 and earlier. You also need to provide a disclosure about Megan's Law (which is a sex offender notification database). My lease has verbiage of this disclosure built within it but if your lease doesn't have this verbiage then you will want an addendum indicating it is the tenant responsibility to review the sex offender database. Addendums required in California are: smoke and carbon monoxide detector addendums. Be sure to know your local ordinances as well. In Santa Cruz we have a noise ordinance so we include a noise addendum. We also live near the coast so we include a mold and mildew addendum. Many local municipalities have special ordinances regarding such things as water restrictions or smoking limitations in buildings. Listed below are other addendums we use:

- Satellite
- Pet
- House Rules
- Renter's Insurance
- Maintenance Instructions
- Tenant Emergency Information Form (Hopefully you won't ever need this information but I have had tenants pass away and I have had to contact relatives.)
- Grilling/BBQ
- Bed Bug
- Move-In/Move-Out detailed reports
- Any rules and regulations that might be required from the Home Owners Association (HOA)
- Parking
- And lastly the owner of the property may have some special notes about the property that should be put into the lease such as how to use the soft water system, the sump pump, care for the wood floors, etc.

To find the most the current legal leases and addendums to use you can Google "property management trade associations." I use the California Association of Realtors (CAR) lease and my addendums come from California Apartment Association (CAA) www.caanet.org.

B

Business, Business Partners – Vendors, Attorneys, Insurance, CPA, & Property Manager

Business

Property owners, landlords, whatever you call yourself, most people forget this very important aspect of property management. I have found that many problems that new (and old) landlords get themselves into arise from not treating their rental as a BUSINESS. They treat it as the home they raised their kids in, the home that they inherited, or their first condo before moving up to a single family home.

Landlords often get themselves into trouble when they become friends with their tenants. They'll allow the tenants to pay rent late, to paint the house, to have pets (when the lease says no pets), to have additional people living in the house, to move in with no security deposit because they will take it in payments and then they never get the payments... the list goes on.

If you approach your rental as a business, with a legal contract between an owner and a tenant and you enforce the contract, then you can have a profitable business with tenants that appreciate having a fair landlord.

But if you aren't good at being a businessperson, then hire a professional property manager to run your business for you. You will make money and be happier in the long run.

Business Partners – Bookkeeper/CPA, Insurance, Attorneys, Maintenance Vendors, & Property Manager

In setting up your business you need others to support you. So think about all of the pieces that you will need.

Bookkeeper/CPA

Have a bookkeeper if you just hate to do accounting. You can hire a bookkeeper quarterly to get things entered into an accounting software such as Quickbooks. They are also able to generate the 1099 forms that you are required by law to send to vendors that you have paid more than $600 per year for services rendered. Your bookkeeper then can have everything ready to give you for when tax season comes around. I'm not saying you can't do this yourself; just remember that it is important to have a separate bank account for your rentals. You should also have a separate credit card. You do NOT want to be commingling your personal monies with your rental business. Keep them separate. Your CPA will love you.

For my personal rentals I do my own bookkeeping. I use MS Excel to keep a running check register for each property. I record both incoming rent checks, and all my outgoing expenses such as mortgages, maintenance, utilities, insurance, taxes, etc. I also have a large envelope for each rental with the address and current year on the front. I toss all receipts into the envelope and at year's end just print my Cash Flow Sheet as I call it and staple it to the front of the envelope. I give the envelopes to my CPA and she handles the rest for me. This allows me to get my taxes done early, which saves me money in accounting expenses. You don't have to have an elaborate system to keep track of your financial records but you do need a system. Mine, for example, only takes an hour or two a month.

Insurance

You need to have the proper insurance on your property. You need a landlord policy and you need to make sure you have liability coverage as well. A landlord policy is different than your homeowner's insurance and is specific to rental properties in what it covers. It is important to have liability coverage in case a vendor or tenant is injured on your rental property. Check with your insurance agent to make sure you are properly covered.

It's a good idea to take a walk around the property to look for any areas that could be a liability such as tall shrubs that enclose the yard that a burglar could hide in, or a lifted cement walkway that could cause someone to trip. You'll also want to make sure that you have proper lighting on the outside of the property, all the windows lock, and that tree limbs aren't touching the structure or the roof as this allows rodents to gain access to house and to help fires spread quickly. There should be cover plates over all electrical plug outlets – yes that seems like common sense but I can't tell you how often I find homes without them. Does the house have Ground Fault Circuit Interrupter (GFCI) plugs next to sources of water like a kitchen or bathroom sink? These are required in California and will protect a tenant from electric shock should they drop an appliance in the water. You'll want to make sure that the water heater is properly strapped and the circuit breaker box is properly labeled in case of an emergency. Your insurance agent might have a list of things to look for when you do your walk about the property.

A pulley system that was used to open and
close a garage door. It was replaced.

Attorney

I don't know about you but I like to think that I will never need
the services of an attorney. But I will say I have come to use their
advice on many occasions. I would recommend that you contact and set up a relationship with an attorney that specializes in
landlord/tenant issues and eviction. You might also want to use
a real estate business attorney to review your situation and see if
creating an LLC for your rental is a good option for you as well
as an estate-planning attorney to create a living revocable trust
for your rental. I can't emphasis the importance of creating a
trust. I know a few situations where the property owner passed
away and there was no trust in place. When this happens the
property goes into probate, which ties it up in court. This costs
money and many times the property has to be sold in order
to cover legal expenses meaning that any heirs might not even
get it in the end. Once you have real estate you need to secure
and protect it. Personally, I have used all these attorneys. I even
hired an attorney to review the small claims court process so I
would be educated should I ever get served by a former tenant.
An attorney can't represent you in small claims court so it was

important for me to know and understand the process should it ever happen.

<u>Maintenance Vendors:</u>

You never know when you will need their services. Form a relationship and work out pricing with a reliable vendor that is available after hours, on weekends, and on holidays because I can guarantee that you will have an emergency at one of these times. You should have an electrician, contractor, handyman, flooring person (carpet, vinyl, tile), painter, roofer, gutter cleaner, carpet cleaner, house cleaner, window cleaner, gardener, tree service, heating and AC vendor, and locksmith all on speed dial or in your favorites on your smart phone. The one very large piece of advice I would give here is to make sure everyone you use is licensed and insured. Please don't use someone just because they are the cheapest in town. Professional business people will cost a bit more but that is because they are professional. They will show up when they promise, are insured (otherwise you could lose your rental in a lawsuit), and will pay for worker's comp if they have employees. You are paying for professional, quality work and insurance. Remember when an emergency happens you will get what cheap has bought you – no service.

A perfect example of an owner being cheap lead me to serve as an expert witness in a court case. A property owner let his tenant's friend climb a tree to remove a limb. The friend fell out of the tree and had major injuries and of course had no insurance. The friend sued to cover medical costs and won. Was it worth it for the property owner to let the tenant do this? No way. Hire a professional. Both with my professional and personal rentals I NEVER allow my residents to do any maintenance on the property. They know to contact me and that I'll get someone out there to do the job without raising their rent the first chance I get. I want residents to report maintenance. It keeps the property in good condition and prevents the possibility of lawsuits.

You should also treat your vendors very well. I give my top vendors bonuses around Christmas time. I pay all my vendors immediately and well within 30 days. During the month of December I make sure to pay all my vendors immediately since they often need the money for the holidays. I also always ask my vendors if they need any money upfront for materials. Through my business I'll throw an annual client appreciation event for my vendors complete with awards to make it fun. Remember, these guys and gals often are working alone and are always responding to emergencies and last minute turnarounds. They like recognition too. I also like to send thank you notes with gas gift cards, which my vendors love since most drive large trucks. When I inspect a property after it has been painted or had new flooring put in I make sure to notice something small and comment on it to the vendor so they know I did look at their work. I give plenty of praise.

If you create a positive and respectful relationship with your vendors you will be able to send them back to make a correction when necessary and they will make it right usually at no cost to you. Cheap companies will go back but charge you. I have seen it plenty of times in my business, I'll recommend a specific carpet cleaner but my tenants will choose to use a cheaper one. It isn't cheaper if you pay for the job twice! Build a positive relationship with your vendors and they will put you before others, which can mitigate further damage to your property in an emergency situation such as a fire, sewage back up, burst water pipe or tree through the roof in a storm. If you treat your vendors with this level of respect and appreciation they will be there when you need them most even if it's 1:00am on a holiday.

Property Manager

A true professional property manager who has been in the business for years and does nothing but property management is worth their weight in gold. For the small monthly management fee you pay them, (which by the way you can write off on your taxes) they manage the accounting for the rental, pay bills, deal with maintenance and vendors (which includes being on call 24/7 for emergencies), ensure the property stays in good condition, deal with tenant issues and possibly with neighbors on such things as fence replacements etc. And of course they manage the process of getting tenants, keeping them, and moving them out all while knowing the laws and keeping the owner of the property out of trouble.

When you need an expert hire an expert. This includes your attorneys, maintenance people and even possibly a property manager. Make sure you have both your "Team" and your residents entered into the contacts of your phone so they are just a call away. This will allow you to be the CEO of your rental business. By being proactive and having options already set up you won't be stressed Googling plumbers as you are boarding a plane for your vacation when an emergency arises. You will make a few simple calls and your team will step in and handle it while you enjoy your vacation.

C

Communicate Clearly, Court – Eviction & Small Claims, Collections, Credit Reports

Communicate Clearly

Communicate clearly, repeatedly, often, and in writing. When I was teaching I learned to tell my students what you are going to do, do it, and then tell them what you did.

In property management I can't begin to tell you how often we repeat the same thing over and over. People only hear a fraction of what you tell them.

In any kind of interaction with a potential tenant all the way through to the day they move out you need to communicate verbally, then followed up with an email or letter that summarizes the conversation and what was agreed to. This way people have time to respond if there is a misunderstanding. Keep all communication in writing because after time two people can remember the same event completely differently. I'm not saying someone is lying, it is just they remember the situation from their perspective.

Communication is written, verbal and non-verbal and visual. Present the info in as many different formats as possible. I take photos of the property before the tenant moves in, I write up a detailed move in report and I allow the tenant to add to the move in report once they have moved into the property. When they move out I again take photos, write a detailed move out report and compare it against the initial move in one. I communicate all the information in a letter accompanied by their security deposit check.

If, you keep your communication clear, detailed, and documented you will have a successful relationship with your landlord or tenant.

Last bit of advice- always try putting yourself in the other person's position so as to understand their point of view. However, never break the rule about following the lease. The lease is a legal contract and the only way to hold someone accountable is to enforce it when necessary. I can tell you from personal experience the few times I have gone out of my way to accommodate someone it has always come back to bite me. An example- the rent is due on the 1st of the month and considered late after the 5th. The tenant calls and tells you they were in a car accident and won't be able to pay the rent until the 7th. Then the 7th comes and goes and now it isn't until the 15th that they can pay you. You need to post a 3-day notice (more on this under N for Notices) when the rent is late and hope they pay on the 7th, if not, then you proceed with the eviction and hiring an eviction attorney.

Court – Eviction & Small Claims

It is never fun to end up in court but if you are going to run a rental business at some point you might end up there. So how do you know when it is time to do an eviction? If the rent is 30 days late, if you have to chase the tenant down, if tenant isn't returning your calls about why the rent is late, or if you have given the tenant notice to move and they are past the move out date then it's time. Thankfully, in my 10 years of property management I have never had to do an eviction but that's mostly due to the thorough screening to get quality tenants. Quality tenants will talk to you if their circumstances have changed and they need to move or can't pay rent.

I have done evictions for clients and usually the situation is the property owner has listened to the tenant's sad story about why the rent is late, then why they weren't able to pay by the agreed upon date, on and on. As time passes the stories just keep getting better. The reality is you are NOT their social worker, therapist or marriage counselor. You are the landlord and the rent is due. By the time the property owner calls me it has been months with no rent and they are just done listening to the reasons why the rent isn't getting paid. If I like the property I will take the job and handle the evictions. Once I have a contract to manage the property we notify the tenants that we are now managing the property and rent is due to us by a certain date. If not, then we proceed with eviction. I tell the owners to not talk with the tenant or return their calls. Usually the tenant will call the property owner and try to negotiate the rent with more stories so they don't have to deal with a professional. Once we are involved the tenant knows the game is up and they will be forced to move.

Should you ever find yourself in this situation you should contact a good eviction attorney, and find out how much they charge to do the eviction. They will ask you for the lease and information about how much rent is owed to you and they will take it from there. When you hear horror stories from owners saying it took 6 months to get a tenant out it is because they were doing the eviction themselves. Once you hire a good eviction attorney the process should take no more than six weeks.

Once I had an owner beg me to take on his property in order to get the tenants out. They hadn't paid rent in over 4 months. He agreed to stay out of the way and pay the $900 in attorney fees. Within a week we had to stop the process because he was talking with the tenants. This owner was so cheap he didn't want to pay the $900 to get the tenants out when at that point he had lost about $6000 in uncollected rent! How foolish. He was willing to lose another $1500 by naively thinking the tenant would now pay. Within the month he called me back but this time I gave him the name of an attorney to use and told him I would be happy to manage the property once the tenant was out. I never heard from him again.

You have to run your rental business like a business. How long will you go carrying the loss until you decide to cut your losses and do something about it? Hire an expert don't do it yourself. I am a professional property manager and I hire an attorney to do the eviction. I don't do it myself.

What you may not know about going to court is that if you get a judgment in your favor for the lost rent, damages, etc. the court can attach the tenant's wages for repayment AND the judgment will now be on their credit report. Once you have a judgment you can also send it to a collection agency and they will pursue the evicted tenants. They keep a percentage, but if the dollar amount is large enough it might be worth it. Their credit report will show an unlawful detainer. What does that mean? It means that in the future they will have an extremely difficult time finding a place to live. However, an unlawful detainer can take up to 60 days to show on a credit report so my tip is to check with the courts from the city or county where a tenant previously lived to see if they have an unlawful detainer on file.

I spend time explaining this to people that are on the verge of being evicted that their credit will be ruined and the eviction will stay on their credit report for a minimum of seven years. You might be able to get them to just leave the property and call it a wash. However, if they owe you months of rent it could be worth going to court.

Collections

Say you have won your award in court, but the tenant has lost their job so there is no income to go after. You can contact a credit bureau and ask to file a collection. This will show on their credit and if they ever want to buy a home it will negatively affect a lot of financial moves they want to make. In some cases the tenant will pay the debt years later just so they can move on. But if they don't, the credit bureau passes the collection to other agencies that will pursue the debt. If the debt is paid it is split with the collection agency and the property owner. In over 10 years I have only had to file two collections on behalf of property owners. Both were related to damages well over the deposit collected and not related to evictions.

So this brings up damages and collections. If you have a tenant that moves but leaves the property damaged make sure to take lots of photos, keep a detailed account of the cost to repair and get the deposit back to tenant with receipts or estimates within the allotted days required by law in your state. For example, in California it is 21 days. Once everything is sent, try to work out a payment with the tenant. Often you will get nothing so at this point you can send the paperwork to collections. If you let the tenant know you will be doing this it might prompt them to pay up but most likely not. Lastly, and very importantly keep the file for four years. Legally, the tenant can come back and contest a held deposit counting on the fact that the paperwork was shred years ago and now you can't prove that they ever got the deposit return paperwork within the 21 days. This happened to me recently.

Credit Reports

You must always run a credit report yourself and never accept an applicant's free credit report. Why? Well the credit report they will provide you reflects revolving credit such as credit cards. It doesn't show if they have any judgments such as an unlawful detainer (eviction), tax liens, or monetary judgments like child support. It will also show if they have had a bankruptcy and whether it is discharged or not.

This is also your first step in qualifying an applicant so you want to do it right. Otherwise you can be setting yourself up for approving someone who may not be qualified and you may have problems down the line. You don't want to end up in court over an eviction. The way I see it is that if they lie about their credit report, then they will lie about their pay stub (verification of income) and everything else on the application such as references, prior landlords, number of occupants, pets etc. Also, fake credit reports can be created. In my career I have seen three fake tax returns. Did you know there are online companies that will provide all kinds of fake documents? Google it and you'll be surprised.

It is best if you run credit reports for all your applicants through the same agency so that you can show you are treating all applicants the same, and thus not discriminating against any one person as per the Fair Housing Act. This is also a great standard reply to anyone who wants to give you their own credit report and doesn't want you to run theirs. In the past I have told people straight up, "Then this isn't the property for you."

So where can you go to run credit? There are many professional trade associations that offer it with membership. In my area we have CAA (California Apartment Association) and you don't have to own an apartment to use them. They have lots of documents for leases and addendums as well. There is another organization in California, AOA (Apartment Owner Association) again you don't have to own an apartment and they offer documentation and credit reporting with their membership. Both these organizations also offer classes on how to be a better landlord and to protect your investment. In my company I provide a service where I will run credit reports and take care of the lease paperwork for clients who show and advertise their property themselves. This situation comes about when the owner lives on site and is renting a granny unit, or a room in their house.

My company uses a credit-reporting agency because of the volume we run. They do an audit on us annually which includes a site visit to make sure we are protecting applicant's information according to the law. I appreciate this level of service and it keeps us on top of our game.

D

Document, Detailed, Due Diligence, Deposits, Damages, Discriminate

Document

You want to document everything in case a tenant or former tenant decides to take you to court or in case the IRS decides to audit your accounting. Use email to cover communication bases. Keep all documentation– receipts, letters, leases, notices, photos– everything.

Detailed

You want to be detailed in your business. Your lease should be very detailed. Your emails should be detailed so there is no chance of miscommunication. Keep accurate records and dates.

Due Diligence

When you are processing an application you need to check everything on the application. Run the credit report yourself because people can change reports or use someone else's (see the Credit Report section for more information). I once had someone give me a fake tax return. Call current and past landlords, check bank statements, call employer and references. Check the driver's license to make sure you have matching names of the person on the application with the person actually in front of you. Check the county court records and public notices for evictions. You can still end up with a problem but if you do your due diligence the chances of getting burned decrease substantially.

Deposits

California law states you can collect 2 times the rent for an unfurnished property and 3 times the rent for a furnished property. Both in my company and in Santa Cruz it is common practice to collect 1.5 times the rent. It is not recommended to collect first, last and a security deposit. Why? I know in the past that was the way it was done but there are some reasons why you only want to collect rent and deposit. Let's say you collect first and last rent and a deposit at a tenant's move in. 20 years later the tenant gives you a 30-day notice to move and says I paid last month's rent. The problem occurs when the rent started at $1,000 at move in and now the rent is $2,000. The last month rent a tenant paid was $1,000, so you lose out on the other $1,000. Legally you can't ask for the balance due on the rent. So you are out of luck. Also, what if the rent first and last plus deposit adds up to more than 2 times the rent? It is illegal to collect more deposit than 2 times the rent. So be safe, just collect rent plus deposit. My recommendation is to make the deposit a different amount than the rent so the tenant doesn't think they paid last month rent. They will give you 30 day notice and say they paid last month and when you remind them they didn't pay last month and still owe rent they will panic. If you are good hearted and decide to use the deposit for the last month rent what happens when they move out and the house isn't returned cleaned? Now you have no funds to do the necessary cleaning and will either have to pay yourself and incur the loss or pay and then take the former tenant to small claims court. My recommendation is rent and a security deposit. If you accept a pet then an extra amount of money should be collected for the pet and then APPLIED to the entire security deposit. It should not be called a pet deposit. Keep in mind if you add extra towards a deposit for pets the total deposit amount cannot exceed the 2 times rent or 3 times rent rule. For more information on pets see the P section on Pets.

Damages

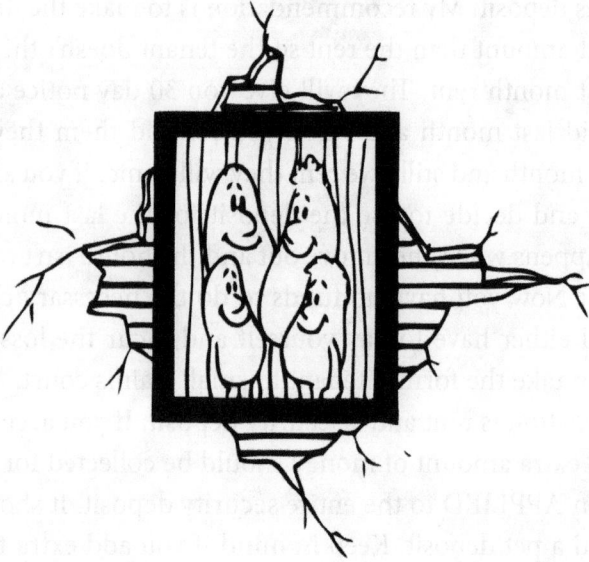

When a tenant moves out the issue of damages versus normal wear and tear sometimes comes up. Here are a few examples: If the entire residence was freshly painted and now the walls have crayon marks all over them, excessive holes from pictures or the tenant repainted the walls without permission you can withhold money to repaint the walls. This is not wear and tear. Normal wear and tear is if you can easily touch up the walls without completely repainting everything such as a few marks on the walls from furniture rubbing. If new carpet was installed and a year later a majority of it is permanently stained you can charge for new carpet and or replace the damaged section if possible. This is not considered wear and tear. Wear and tear is a few small stain spots near the kitchen, or dirt marks in front of the entry front door.

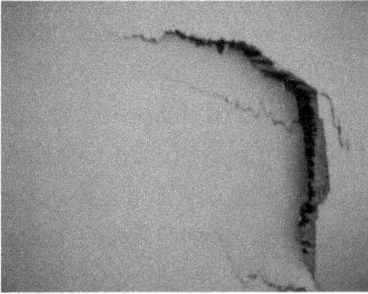

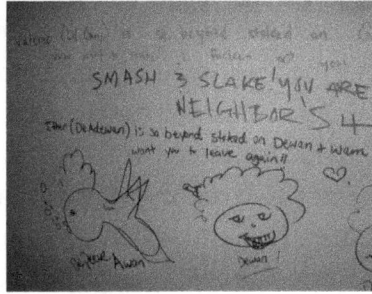

**Walls that are broken through or drawn on are
not considered normal wear and tear.**

The bottom line is if you withhold for damages you must return the security deposit minus the charges for damages within 21 days from the date you received the keys. (This is for California – check your states laws since they are all different.) If the deposit isn't returned within 21 days the tenant is entitled to double their security deposit. They can and will take you to small claims court to get their deposit plus back. Tenants win the majority of small claims court actions because owners fail to return deposits within the 21 days as required by law. The packet that you send to the departing tenant must have an itemized list of income (deposit you hold) plus interest on the deposit (if required by law in your area) and expenses (deductions from the deposit). It should also include copies of receipts for the amounts withheld to repair the damages, photos taken both before and after the occupancy, and copies of both the move in and the move out reports to document the damages. The question I get is, "What do I do if I won't be able to get all the repairs done within the 21 days?" You have to provide an estimate of all the charges against the deposit and include estimates from vendors. Hold back that amount and send the balance of the deposit to the tenant (if there is a balance) within the 21 days. Let the tenant know as soon as the work is done you will send a revised and final accounting. You must do this as soon as possible; the work shouldn't take months to do.

As long as you document the condition of the property and provide the tenant with copies of everything you can withhold money to cover damages. I always ask people, "What would a judge say if you ended up in small claims court?" I have never (knock on wood) had to go to court over a deposit return. This is because I DOCUMENT everything in DETAIL and because I do my DUE DILIGENCE before a tenant moves in.

Discriminate

The Fair Housing Act of 1988 states:

It is illegal to discriminate against any person because of Race, Color, Religion, Sex, Handicap, Familial Status, or National Origin.

I highly recommend that you take a Fair Housing class. These classes are offered through rental/property management trade associations and are usually only a half-day. I send my staff annually. We all return to the office with knees knocking and scared to answer the phone once we hear examples of lawsuits filed by HUD for discrimination, but it makes us mentally sharp and reminds us to be ever vigilant in what we say and do so as to not discriminate. Here are a few examples to share with you. I know a property management company in my area that didn't have a receptionist and the property managers would answer the phone. What is wrong with this? A receptionist consistently answers the phone the same way each time. So, a call came in and property manager 1 picked up the phone and spent a great deal of time answering all of the caller's questions (this property manager may have had the time to do this) a second call came in and property manager 2 picked up the phone and redirected the person to the company website (this property manager may have been very busy at the time of the call). A lawsuit was filed against the company for discrimination against the caller because of the caller's language accent. It turns out that the same person called the office twice, and during the second call spoke with an accent. They claimed that because of the accent they were redirected to the website for information. This sounds crazy but not only did the property management company pay a $25,000 fine to settle the complaint, but most likely their insurance premium rose because a lawsuit had been filed and was now on record.

Another example includes an apartment owner who showed their property. The applicant asked if there were any kids in the complex and the owner said, "No" A lawsuit was filed because the applicant felt the owner was discriminating against families and the owner of the property ended up paying $250,000 in damages. These lawsuits are real and we hear about them in our Fair Housing training. We can't let fear rule our lives we just need to be vigilant and careful in what we say and do at all times.

Even the words you use in advertising your rental can be discriminatory. We briefly touched on this under Advertising and I will cover it in detail under Screening Applicants.

E

Evaluate & Efficient

Evaluate

When a property comes vacant you always need to evaluate how much to do on a property during a turnover between tenants. You need to evaluate if the property needs to be upgraded to make it more current and appealing to a current renter's wants and needs. An example would be an older home without a dishwasher in the kitchen. If it is an apartment I might say, no, because if you put one dishwasher in you will need to put in all units. But in a single family home you would want to put a dishwasher in. Not only do moms and families today expect a dishwasher but you can also get more rent for providing one.

Paint is cheap so always make sure the walls are freshly painted. Replacing carpet and vinyl flooring are the easiest ways to upgrade a property that will give big returns on the dollar. I can tell you I have done tenant placement (which means I find the tenant for the owner and the owner then manages the property) for some owners who refuse to replace carpet and are willing to take lower rent... yes I have seen green shag carpet from the 70's it is still out there. My recommendation and rule is:

Would you live here? If you wouldn't live with shag, why would you have this expectation for your tenant?

Evaluation always comes down to return on the dollar and keeping the property in good shape. If the counters are old but in good condition don't change them out. If the vinyl flooring is from 1970's then change it. Take down drapes and put up blinds. Take out old light fixtures and put in newer ones. These are simple and cost effective changes that will return a real bang for the buck.

Efficient

When showing properties you want to be efficient with your time. Screen people over the phone so you know if they can afford the property and if it will be a good fit. People don't always read the ad they just see the price and call. It doesn't do anyone any good to set up a showing appointment only to have them ask you if you will take $600.00 less a month because they can't afford the rent or they thought you took pets when the ad clearly said, "No Pets." Don't do showings daily. Why? Because you will have lots of people who will not show up and now you have just wasted a couple hours of your day. I assume you have better things to do with your time than sit at a vacant rental property. Group multiple applicants together when you show a property. If they are really interested they will apply if they see others interested. It also allows you to manage your time better. Pick a showing time and make people conform to you. Don't keep changing your schedule for each applicant; your time is worth something. It will also help you to be less upset when people cancel without telling you. When I set appointments I tell the applicant they must call me back within one hour of the showing to confirm or I don't show. You wouldn't believe the people that never confirm but it sure saved me time and frustration sitting at a property and having a no show. Lastly, keep in mind if potential renters can't follow your simple instructions of: drive by property first to see if they like the neighborhood, show up on time at a showing, provide you with a complete application and supporting documentation such as pay stubs, then what makes you think they will follow the lease? They won't!

E's are important!

F

Filing System, Fair Housing Laws, Friends & Family

<u>Filing System</u>

To be organized and to be able to document everything associated with managing a rental you need a filing system and it doesn't really matter what system you use - just have one. I will tell you what I have both personally and in my business.

For my personal rentals I use a binder to keep the lease, maintenance log, and communication log (this includes email communication, and phone conversations). I use a binder so I can quickly find all of the things I need to know most. I also have a file cabinet with a file for each property where invoices, bills, insurance, property taxes, and mortgage statements are stored.

In my business we have locked file cabinets with a file for every property that has 5 dividers in it. Each section is labeled- Tenant, Owner, Invoices, Communication, and Misc. General Info. We also have a separate owner file if an owner has many properties. All files are locked up daily. We have online file folders with each property address and an owner file. This is where we put all scanned documents, communication with tenants and owners and any items that get emailed to us. We scan all leases and management contracts so we have those online as well. All invoices are scanned and emailed with owner statements monthly.

If you're managing your own property I recommend keeping your filing system easy and simple so you will actually use it. I started out with complex spreadsheets but then simplified to a bank ledger method that listed each entry just like you would in a checkbook. I print this list at the end of the year and give it to my CPA. It is stapled to the front of an envelope for the property with all the documentation, receipts, etc. inside so that an accountant may review for more detail.

Fair Housing Laws

You need to know the law. California, for example, is a tenant right's state. This means judges lean toward the rights of tenants and in most court cases will rule for the tenant. If you follow the Fair Housing Laws you will stay out of trouble and out of court. On the first page of my application I have a paragraph that reads as follows:

Management welcomes all applicants and supports the precepts of equal access and "Fair Housing." Management will not refuse access to any housing, accommodation, or other interest in property or otherwise discriminate against an applicant on the basis of age, sex, race, religion, marital/familial status, physical or mental handicap, color, creed, ethnicity, national origin or sexual orientation.

I state Fair Housing laws everywhere– in my office, in my management contracts, and as above on the first page of my applications. I have also printed the Fair Housing Laws and have them framed and on the wall of our office in the reception area and again in our display case mounted on the outside of our building where people pick up listings of properties. By doing this it publicly states that we are a company that follows ALL Fair Housing Laws. We state this regularly over the phone to people who may get upset with us for example when we state we can't show a property that day because the property is tenant occupied and we are required to provide 24-hour notice. You wouldn't believe the people that get angry with us and then post a negative review on Yelp stating, "This company refused to show us a property." They neglect to state that we are bound by Fair Housing laws that stipulate we MUST give tenant-24 hour notice and we offered to set up a showing another day convenient for them.

I have taken many classes on this topic and I would recommend you do the same. The CAA (California Apartment Association) offers classes on this topic at www.caanet.org or for more info about Fair Housing https://portal.hud.gov/hudportal/HUD?src=/program_offices/fair_housing_equal_opp.

People break Fair Housing Laws all the time and as a person and company that is bound by these laws here is an example of a real situation I had with one of my property owners. I once had an elderly owner that lived in a duplex and I found the perfect tenant for the unit next door. The potential tenant had perfect credit, met all the criteria to rent, but had a toddler. The owner refused to rent to them because of the child. This is against the law. I advised the owner that they were breaking the law but they refused and stated it was their property they could rent to whomever they wanted and they didn't want kids. I informed the owner of the potential consequences. I immediately closed my account with this owner, and drove to the duplex, knocked on the door and handed the owner the keys and the final statement. I also advised the applicants that they were well within their right to file a complaint. They didn't- being the nice people that they were.

The government agency Housing and Urban Development (HUD) will also send "testers" to ensure people aren't discriminating. I know of a very good property management company that had to settle a claim of discrimination for $25,000 (if you read the Discrimination section you'll be familiar with this story). What had happened was that an interested party called the office asking about rentals and the person answering the phone spent a lot of time with the caller. Then the caller called back but this time with an accent and asked for rental info. A different staff member answered the phone and referred the person to the company website to preview what they had available. The caller, a tester from HUD, sued the management company saying that because of the language accent they were discriminated against. The caller won and the company settled.

Fair Housing must be taken seriously and you need to know the law. If you work with a property manager they need to know the law, and if you are a property manager you BETTER know the law since you are representing the owner of the property. Property managers have a higher burden to bear and rightly so.

Friends & Family

Never rent to friends and family. I have seen too many times that the idea seems good at the time but it almost always causes the relationship to be strained or outright ruined. Are you really going to evict your friend or family member if they don't pay the rent? Are you going to raise the rent on a regular basis? Just don't do it. Remember this is a business and it is never a good idea to comingle those relationships. I have stated that as a landlord you shouldn't become friends with tenants you are the landlord. It is a professional relationship and should stay that way.

G

Good Perspective, Good Owner, Gardener

I teach classes on how to be a good landlord and what is interesting to me is how often people like to share their horror stories. But what my students fail to realize is that they are part of the relationship. I find that when owners come from a perspective that all tenants are evil, their approach will be adversarial and thus they will reap what they have sown. So I want to address a few of the following G topics.

Good Perspective

Not all tenants are bad; in fact 99% of tenants are good. Approach potential tenants with respect, a friendly disposition, and the view that they are going to be the best tenant you have ever had.

Good Owner

Be good and be responsible. When tenants report a maintenance issue be responsible and fix it. Show you care for the property and address tenant's issues within reason. By trying to solve a problem together you will create a good relationship and hopefully have a long-term tenant.

Gardener

If you have a landscaped property include a gardener with the rent. Tenants say they love to garden but I have yet to see a yard kept up. When I get a landscaper who is looking to rent from me they typically ask for a rent discount if they do the yard work. I ask them to give me a bid for the work. If it is reasonable I will pay them to do it but I won't discount rent. The response I have ALWAYS gotten is, "Then I don't want to do it." That is fine. The point here is to never discount the rent in exchange for the tenant performing the work.

WACK-A-MOLE
5¢

I personally love to include gardeners with the property. It is worth the money to keep the property looking good, plus it is a second set of eyes on the property. My gardeners tell me if there are too many cars at the property, if there is a pet that isn't supposed to be there, or if there is any outdoor maintenance that needs to be done. Living in Santa Cruz we have many people that grow marijuana and they are able to get medical cards to do so. If tenants know there is a gardener and someone on the property regularly they are more than likely not going to apply to rent from me if they have ulterior motives.

If you are going to require the tenant to maintain the yard do not provide the lawn mower or other tools. The reason is if a tenant injures themself using the lawn mower they could sue you for not showing them how to properly use the machine. Tenants will need to provide their own equipment or better yet, hire a gardener!

Be good!

H

Hands-On

When prospective clients call me to ask about my services one of the questions they always ask is if I am "hands-on."

"Hands-on" is a word that has many meanings depending upon who is asking it. My answer is: yes, you want to be hands-on but not a micro-manager. My tag line for my business is: Responsive, Reliable, Common Sense Management. You want to be responsive to tenant requests– especially maintenance issues. If you aren't responsive, then they will stop reporting issues and then the house can really go downhill and you will have that horror story when they move out.

You want to be hands-on throughout the entire management cycle of the rental. You are the one that needs to interview the potential renter over the phone, schedule a showing, personally show the property, and accept the application. You need to verify the info on the application, and approve the applicant. Then you need to prepare the lease and the property for the move in. It is your responsibility to sit down and review the lease with the tenant. Do a move in walkthrough and call the tenant every now and then to see if things are going ok for them. Don't take the attitude that no news is good news.

During move out you especially want to be hands-on during the last month to make sure things go smoothly. You want to make sure you agree upon showing times while the current tenant is still in the property, that they know what is expected of them regarding cleaning to get their full deposit back. I provide a cleaning checklist (which can be found at the end of this section), and vendors such as a carpet and window cleaner so my tenants know whom to use. I also offer a pre-inspection (which is required by California law) during the last two weeks of the tenant's occupancy to walkthrough the unit and come to agreement as to what needs to be done in order for a tenant to get their full refund.

I do the final move out walkthrough alone after I have received the keys from the tenant. I fill out the move out report (I do a move in report and I compare it against the move out report). I take many photos and I schedule any work that might be a charge to a tenant's deposit. I make sure to always get their deposit back to them within 21 days from when they give me the keys.

Keep in mind that hands-on doesn't mean you can be at the property daily, or without 24-hour notice. It means being involved but not overbearing.

If this is too much personal contact for you or just too much work for the time you have then hire a professional property manager and ask them the question, "Are you hands-on?"

Move out Cleaning Checklist

Kitchen
- ☐ Work area.
- ☐ Clean in/outside cupboard doors, remove fingerprints etc. Polish.
- ☐ Clean cupboard shelves and inside drawers.
- ☐ Clean cupboard under sink and remove all products.
- ☐ Clean counters and remove stains.
- ☐ Clean sink, remove stains, and polish fixtures.
- ☐ Clean wall around and above sink.

Stove
- ☐ Clean walls around and above stove.
- ☐ Clean in/outside hood and fan.
- ☐ Remove filter, clean; put back.
- ☐ Clean outside panels and door handle.
- ☐ Clean control panel.
- ☐ Clean oven and racks.
- ☐ Clean storage drawer(s).
- ☐ Clean broiler pan (if supplied).
- ☐ Clean stove top and rings.
- ☐ Clean drip pans or replace them.

Refrigerator

☐ Remove all food. Clean sides, top, door & handles.
☐ Defrost and clean freezer.
☐ Remove and clean shelves and crisper(s).
☐ Clean door shelves and egg tray.
☐ Clean magnetic seal on/around door(s).
☐ Leave refrigerator plugged in and on.
☐ Remember to remove all products from refrigerator.

Dishwasher

☐ Remove items fallen to the bottom.
☐ Remove soap deposit.
☐ Clean along inside of door edges and hinges.
☐ Clean outside door and control panel.

Floors

☐ Wash and wax.

Bathrooms

☐ Clean tub and tub surround, polish fixtures.
☐ Clean sink and soap holder.
☐ Clean in/outside cupboards and drawers.
☐ Clean medicine cabinet, in/out remove personal belongings.
☐ Clean mirror(s).
☐ Clean in/out/around toilet, remove from tank any dye dispenser/tablet, disinfectant.
☐ Wash floor, remove dirt and grime along tub and toilet base.

General Cleaning

☐ Remove all nails from walls (DO NOT FILL OR TOUCH UP PAINT).

☐ Remove marks and fingerprints on walls.

☐ Clean baseboards.

☐ Dust and clean mini blinds.

☐ Clean windowsills, tracks, in/outside glass.

☐ Clean closet shelves and rods.

☐ Remove cobwebs.

☐ Wash all tile/vinyl floors.

☐ Have carpets PROFESSIONALLY cleaned.

Light Fixtures

☐ Dust light fixtures. Remove cover, wash, put back in place.

☐ Clean light bulbs and replace burnt out light bulbs.

☐ Clean switch plates and replace any broken or missing plates.

Fireplace/Wood Stove/Insert

☐ Remove debris and clean.

☐ Clean hearth and mantle.

☐ Clean around wall areas.

Smoke Detector/Alarm(s)

☐ Test alarm(s) and replace batteries if necessary. Retest to insure working order.

Outside

☐ Remove cobwebs from eaves and doorways.

☐ Clean exterior fixtures and replace burnt out bulbs.

☐ Wedge and weed all flowerbeds.

☐ Mow lawn(s).

☐ Remove all debris from grounds and storage area.

☐ Remove all personal belongings from outside.

☐ Broom and clean the garage.

☐ Remove all garbage, recyclable and yard waste containers. Must be left clean if staying with the property.

Repairs

☐ Repair any tenant damage done to the property.

☐ Replace any broken windows.

Last

Please remove all personal belongings. Management will not be responsible for any items left behind. It will be hauled to the dump at tenants' expense. Do a final walkthrough by yourself(s) to double check the list.

ALL ITEMS NOT COMPLETED WILL BE CHARGED TO THE TENANT(S) once keys are turned into office; Security deposit is returned within 21 days (as is required by California law).

Vendor Recommendations:

Tenant Signature: X

Tenant Signature: X

Tenant Signature: X

I

Inspections & Insurance

Inspections

So how often should you do inspections and how detailed should they be? You should always do a detailed inspection with photos prior to tenant move in. Drive-bys throughout the year are fine. If the yard is looking shabby you might want to schedule an inside inspection or send the tenant a quick note that the yard is looking shabby. This lets them know you do check on the property.

I think it is reasonable to let your tenant know you will be doing an annual inspection. I would use the same checklist annually. To be most effective, schedule annual inspections and have them done by a handyman or contractor. But remember, you must give the tenant a 24-hour notice. By using an outside source you will get a better assessment of the property. They can also always do quick, easy repairs on the spot. By using an outside person the tenant is more relaxed. You can also potentially find out if there are pets on the property if the lease says no pets, or can see if there are more people living in the property than what is stated on the lease. You can also ask the vendor to let you know overall cleanliness of the property.

If the owner or property manager does the inspection, the tenant gets a 24-hour notice and the place gets cleaned up prior to you showing up. In my business I rarely do the inspection during a tenancy, I have my maintenance manager do it. We keep the maintenance checklist in the file so we have a record of the maintenance history. I always do the move out inspection and again take photos. This alleviates disputes with security deposit and it keeps you informed as to the condition of the property. You get to see it with your own eyes.

Keep in mind tenants must get a 24-hour notice for any inspection (inside or outside property) and inspections shouldn't be done monthly or even quarterly. When I do meet with property owners they often ask me if I can go inside the property monthly or quarterly to check on it. My response is the tenant might feel you are spying on them. A reasonable way to get into the property is to check batteries in detectors, which you can do twice per year. Perform a more detailed annual maintenance check. If you allow pets in the property write into your lease that you will do pet inspections twice a year. Now you have been in the property at least 3 times in 12 months. Tenants pay rent and have a right to quiet enjoyment of the property.

I would also say it isn't ok to walk up and down the sidewalk or drive-by daily. If you do get out of the car and are going to step on to the property you legally must give the tenant 24 hour notice. Put yourself in your tenant's shoes. How would you feel if your landlord was showing up all the time? If as a property owner you just worry too much about the property consider hiring a property manager or selling the property. It is ok, not everyone is meant to be a landlord.

Insurance

Insurance should be reviewed annually. Owners need a landlord policy and if the property is a condo the owner needs their own insurance in addition to insurance they may pay as part of their HOA fees. I am always surprised at how many owners don't carry insurance and are under the false assumption that the HOA will cover any damages. It is also recommended that tenants have renter's insurance. It is incredibly cheap - on average $120 per year and it protects the tenant in case there is a fire or flood or any other reason the residence is damaged and unable to be occupied. In addition, renter's insurance will also cover theft of belongings. The tenant needs to check on what their policy covers and of course it is dependent upon what type of coverage they are willing to pay for. I have rented to people who lost everything in a fire and they had renters insurance, which covered their hotel costs, paid for new furnishings, and clothes and even paid their deposit on the rental and the first month's rent. I was shocked at the level of coverage. I am truly convinced that all tenants should have renter's insurance. After hearing tenants cry over losses and seeing what can be covered by renter's insurance my business now requires renter's insurance for all of our tenants and proof of it must be given to us before the tenant moves in.

J

Jaded, Job, Judge, Judge Others

<u>Jaded</u>

I have seen long time property owners who have gotten to a point where they become jaded about tenants and being a landlord. The landlord starts to dread getting calls from the tenant and usually assumes the worst case scenario when the phone rings such as the toilet is backing up, or the rent will be late. Owning the rental property has become a burden emotionally. This ultimately comes about because the owners don't have procedures in place so every interaction with their tenants is a new and taxing experience. This is when property owners will often seek out professionals to take over management. After a lifetime of being a landlord, they are now at the point where they don't want to spend their free time taking care of maintenance, showing the property, doing the paperwork and the accounting. Personally I believe these owners should start enjoying the fruits of their labor and consider hiring a professional property manager.

Job

Managing real estate should be viewed as a job. I often deal with property owners who have either inherited their property, or decide to rent out their old condo after upgrading to a different home. Since there is usually an attachment to the property, the owners usually never go into landlording with an investor's business mind. Like any investment, the management of rentals should be taken seriously and as a job. It should ultimately earn you money or help you achieve some future financial goal. If it becomes a financial or emotional drain, then that is when an owner gets into trouble.

Judge

There's "judge" like the person in the courtroom and "judge" as in judging others. Both are important to touch upon but let's discuss the one in the black robe first.

Anytime owners end up before a judge, whether it's because they are evicting a tenant or the tenant is suing them over charges to their security deposit, there is stress and frustration. Most small claims court cases, such as a dispute over the security deposit, end with the owner losing, so add in loss of time, energy and even more frustration. The best way to stay out of court is to follow the lease, and enforce it. Keep accurate and detailed records, move in reports, take photos, and have a detailed communication log with tenants and vendors. Always try to find a resolution that will create a win/win situation for everyone. I always tell owners to put themselves in the judge's shoes and ask, "What would the judge say?" If you follow the law and document everything you will be fine. It is often better to help the tenant move on and to find something they can afford. You have two choices if the tenant isn't paying rent on time. One option is to post a 3-day notice to pay rent or quit, which means they must pay the rent within 3 days or the eviction process starts. But think about it, if they don't have money to pay rent, they don't have money to move. The second option that has worked for me is to come to an agreement with them; you are willing to give the tenant half of their deposit upfront so they have money to put down on a new place, and if they move out on time and leave the unit clean, you will give them the remaining deposit within 24 hours instead of within the 21 days required by California law. Please remember to double-check the required dates within your own state. The few times I have done this I have had excellent results. The tenant doesn't want to not pay, they just can't. By treating them with respect and understanding their financial situation, you will have a very positive outcome.

Judge Others

Well, don't. You cannot afford to judge others. If Fair Housing laws are violated you could end up paying very stiff fines that can run into hundreds of thousands of dollars (just read some of the horror stories in section F under Fair Housing). As long as applicants meet your qualifications they can rent your property. Let me share with you a personal story. Santa Cruz, CA, where I have my business, is a very tolerant and alternative community. I was once showing a property on a rainy day when a young woman in her mid-twenties showed up. She was all in black including her hair, had lots of piercings in her ears, nose and lip. She offered to take her shoes off since it was raining. As she entered the unit I noticed she had tattoos on the top of her feet. My first thoughts were "Ouch!" whereas someone else could have said, "This is not the kind of tenant I want..." When she applied, we processed her and approved her. Her stats were great: high income, steady long-term job, extremely high credit score, and raving reviews from prior landlords. She turned out to be one of our favorite tenants and in two years gave notice because she had just bought her first home. We were thrilled for her. If we had judged her by appearance only, we would have missed out on a wonderful tenant and person. What is that old saying, "Never judge a book by its cover," how true!

K

Keys

What are your policies and procedures for keys? Whatever they are, be sure to have a coding system for your keys, a secure place to keep them and always re-key the property:

I am often amazed at how many property owners don't want to re-key between tenants. Here is my argument for doing so.

1. You have no idea how many keys are floating around or who has them.
2. You are assuming a huge liability if anything were to happen to a new tenant.
3. A tenant can't get renter's insurance without the unit being re-keyed.
4. It isn't expensive to re-key In our area the trip charge is $75 and each key is $1.00.
5. It allows you to have a locksmith inspect all knobs and locks for security.
6. Housing codes change. For example, some older properties have deadbolts, which require a key to unlock from the inside. These are now against building codes and need to be changed out or a permanent key installed on the inside deadbolt.
7. You set the tone for the tenant that you treat your property as a business, and that you are willing to spend money to do maintenance and care for their welfare.

8. So bottom line - please rekey in between tenants.

If you have multiple properties have a coding system on the key tag- never the property address in case the key gets lost or stolen. Always have keys in a secure place within your home such as a safe or locked drawer. You also want to have a statement in your rental agreement about what happens if a tenant locks themselves out of the rental. Are you going to drive to the property to open the house for them or do they call a locksmith? Think about this because from personal experience it is no fun to get a call from your tenant at 2:00am because they are locked out after a night of fun.

L

Law, Lease, Listen

Law

Bottom line follow it. There are lots of books out there and professional associations here are some links:

1. California Apt Assoc. Become a member. This is a great organization. They regularly have classes on legal matters, Fair Housing Law, Leases and Addendums to download etc. www.caanet.org
2. Institute for Real Estate Management- IREM www.irem.org
3. National Association of Residential Property Managers - NARPM. Become a member. I am very active in this organization. It is geared towards property managers but if you treat your 1 rental like a business then this is a place for you. There are area chapters throughout the US, professional designations, classes, conferences etc. www.narpm.org
4. Apartment Owner Association- AOA -www.aoausa.com
5. Nolo Press has a series of books. I have them on my bookshelves. www.nolo.com

Please look in your state for professional associations to join.

Top Ten Legal Mistakes That Can Sink Your Landlord Business

by Attorney Janet Portman

Know the laws in your state before you rent out space.

Being a successful landlord requires lots of practical know-how, business moxie, and familiarity with the market. Until about 30 years ago, the law didn't have much to do with it. Now, however, federal law and most states closely regulate nearly every aspect of your business. Not knowing the rules can land you in lots of legal hot water.

1. Using Generic or Outdated Lease Forms

Most landlords know it's important to have a written lease or rental agreement. But using the wrong form can get you into trouble. So-called "standard" forms that are sold everywhere probably aren't compliant with the laws in your state. If you use a stationery store lease that short-cuts tenants' rights, you could find yourself at the losing end of a lawsuit because of an unenforceable lease clause. On the other hand, some standard forms actually impose greater obligations and restrictions on you than your state's law does! (My favorite requires landlords to return security deposits within ten days, which no state requires.)

2. Asking the Wrong Questions During Applicant Screening

Thorough tenant screening is the most important part of your business – if you choose poorly, you're in for nothing but headaches, with tenants who don't pay the rent, trash your place, or worse. But there are limits to what you can ask. Many landlords don't realize that even well-meaning questions (such as asking a disabled person about his disability or asking if a couple is married) can be illegal forms of discrimination. If the applicant doesn't get the rental, even though your rejection had nothing to do with the offending question, that disappointed tenant has ammunition for a fair housing complaint (which fair housing watch-dog groups are eager to pursue).

3. Setting Policies that Discriminate Against Families

Although it's been illegal to discriminate against families for over 20 years, many owners' practices are far from family-friendly – and are downright illegal. Excluding families because you feel children cause more wear and tear and you prefer a "mature, quiet" environment is illegal. And while you're permitted to limit the number of residents in a unit (in most situations, two occupants per bedroom), you may not apply that standard differently when dealing with families. The cost of this mistake can be another trip to your lawyer's office, to deal with a fair housing complaint.

4. Making Promises That You Don't Deliver On

It's fine to he enthusiastic about the benefits of your property, and it's necessary to do so in competitive markets, but understand that your enthusiastic promises will become binding if applicants rely on them when deciding to rent. For example, you may have to deliver the goods if you assure an applicant of a parking space, satellite service or a new paint job. A tenant who feels ripped off may legally break the lease or sue you for the difference in value between what he was promised and what you delivered. Whether the tenant will win is hardly the point – you'll have to respond, which will cost time and money.

5. Charging Excessive Late Fees

Late fees can be a powerful tool to motivate tenants to pay the rent on time. And while a higher fee can be a better motivator, some landlords cross the line, by setting fees that bear little resemblance to the actual damages they suffer when tenants pay late. Courts are increasingly invalidating excessive late fees that can't be justified with hard evidence. You're better off setting a modest fee that reflects your true damages, and dealing with chronic late-payers with pay-or-quit notices.

6. Violating Tenants' Rights to Privacy

Most states have detailed rules on when, for what reasons, and with how much notice you may enter a tenant's home. Yet many landlords stop by unannounced, asking to check things over, perform an on-the-spot repair, or show the place to prospective tenants. Repeated violations of a tenant's privacy (or even one outrageous violation) can excuse a tenant from any further obligations under the lease and may also result in court-ordered money damages against the landlord.

7. Using Security Deposits for the Wrong Projects

The most frequent types of cases heard in small claims court are arguments over security deposit retentions. Yet the basic rule – that deposits should be used only to cover damage beyond wear and tear, needed cleaning, and unpaid rent – isn't hard to understand. Still, landlords routinely use the deposit to cover appliance upgrades, cosmetic improvements and other refurbishing, not repairs. Not surprisingly, many of these landlords lose these cases in small claims court.

8. Ignoring Dangerous Conditions In and Around the Rental

Landlords in virtually every state are required to offer and maintain housing that meets basic health and safety standards, such as those set by state and local building codes, health ordinances, and landlord-tenant laws. If you fail to take care of important repairs, deal with environmental hazards, or respond when your property has become an easy mark for criminals, tenants may break the lease and, in many states, withhold the rent or make the repair themselves and deduct the expense from the rent. Landlords who have failed to make their properties reasonably secure in the face of repeated on-site crime are often ordered to compensate the tenant-victim when yet another criminal intrudes. These are expensive ways to learn the law.

9. Keeping Security Deposits When Tenants Break a Lease

When tenants break a lease and leave early; landlords often keep the entire deposit, reasoning that the tenant 's bad behavior justifies doing so, and that they'll ultimately need it anyway to cover rent. In many states, this is illegal – you must take reasonably prompt steps to re-rent, and credit any new rent toward the tenant's obligation for the rest of the lease. Keeping a two months' rent deposit and re-renting within a month is not legal.

10. Failing to Return Security Deposits According to Law

This list wouldn't be complete without another reference to security deposits. Not only are they used improperly, they' re often not returned according to state law, either. Many states have deadlines by which landlords must itemize their use of the deposit and return any balance. It's not uncommon for tenants to wait many weeks or months for this accounting. In some states, the deliberate or "bad faith" retention of the deposit will result in harsh penalties against the landlord, such as an order that the landlord pay two or three times the deposit to the tenant.

Lease

Have a current and legal lease. You can get wonderful leases and all kinds of rental forms that are regularly updated by attorneys through www.caanet.org, or www.aoausa.com (both are for California only). It's worth the money to become a member. Each state has their own landlord associations so please become a member.

So what is the difference between a lease and a rental agreement? A lease has a specific start and end date. A rental agreement would be a month to month agreement where you have a start date and no specific end date. Once you have a lease in place you cannot add or remove anything from the lease until the end date is up. Most leases have a provision if the lease is not formally renewed it will automatically become a month to month rental agreement. I always put into our leases that a formal written 30-day notice is required by the tenant if they are going to move. I don't want the tenant to show up on the last day of the lease and give me keys when I had no idea they were moving.

In addition to your lease/rental agreement there are usually a number of addendums that are added to cover all the important information a tenant should know and agree upon. Some addendums are required by local, state, or federal law. For example the City of Santa Cruz has a noise ordinance so we have a Noise Addendum that outlines the law and the fines.

Other standard addendum would cover things such as:

- Lead disclosures (federal law requires this addendum),
- Mold & mildew issues
- Pets
- Use of BBQ's,
- Rules and Regulation by HOA's (Home Owner Associations)
- Parking
- Water restrictions
- Satellite usage
- Smoke & Carbon Monoxide Detector Addendums (required by State of California law)
- A detailed Move-in Report
- Maintenance Instructions
- A Maintenance Request Form

The complete lease that I use in my professional business is 40 pages. I always provide the rental agreement/lease to the tenant a week before they move in so they can read it ahead of time and ask any questions. Never have a tenant sign the lease the day of the move in. Move in day is already very stressful and a tenant won't like being surprised by something unexpected in the lease.

On our move in day with a tenant they are picking up keys and providing us the final move in monies. The lease has already been signed ahead of time. This allows us to have a quick interaction and they are on their way.

Listen

I can't stress this enough. If you look at your rental as a business and try to remove your emotions, you will be a more successful landlord. As owners who previously lived in the property we are willing to over-look certain things (like the leaky faucet in the bathroom) but when you rent the property it needs to be acceptable to the tenant. You need to follow all health and safety laws, such as making sure the windows aren't painted shut and can open for an emergency exit should there be a fire. After all, tenants are paying money to live there and expect things to work properly without a jerry-rigged fix. So make sure that all of the electrical outlets have cover plates and remember to fix the skylight that drips when it rains. It is unacceptable to tell the tenant to put a pan under the dripping spot. By actively listening you will build a good relationship and have good communication with your tenant.

M

Management – Time, Money, Maintenance, Relationships

<u>Time</u>

This is extremely important if you are going to manage your properties yourself. Prospective tenants especially can gobble up and waste your time. The best tip I can give is to get applicants and tenants to work within your schedule. I don't do open houses for showings- you will get nothing but Lookie-Lous. I always set a specific time and I tell an applicant to call me to reconfirm 1 hour before the scheduled showing time. If I do not get confirmation I do not show up. This has saved me a lot of time and keeps me from getting angry over the inconsiderateness of many people. It keeps me from having negative thoughts about renters in general.

You also need to manage your time when it comes to the bookkeeping and paperwork of your rental. I would take out your calendar and schedule out the entire year all the things related to your rental. This includes insurance, taxes, inspections, accounting, and checking in with your vendors to name a few. By scheduling all your landlording tasks ahead of time, you will be able to control and run your business smoothly instead of always being in reactive mode with requests from the tenants, the vendors, your accountant and your insurance agent. I can't stress the time savings you will reap.

Time management is really people management, and this includes yourself.

Money

You need to have a budget and you need to set aside money monthly for taxes, insurance, maintenance, and vacancy. If you don't, you will be stressed and in panic when you get an emergency call that the water heater has gone out. Do you have the $1,000 needed to buy and install a new one? You will get stressed when you get the 30-day notice the tenant is moving out. Did you keep the security deposit in a separate account or did you spend it? Can you afford to not get rent for 30 days during turnover? Do you have some reserves for turnover maintenance?

Owning rental property is expensive and you need to know your long-range goals for why you have this property. In today's current market in Santa Cruz, CA it is rare to have positive cash flow on a rental. So, how long are you willing to invest your own money into this property to reach your goals? Bottom line, you need a budget and you need to follow it.

Maintenance

Here too you need a plan. You need to know how long you have before the roof will need to be replaced. You need to have a plan to do regular maintenance such as annual gutter cleaning and replacing smoke detector batteries. Many owners feel that if they don't hear from the tenants then things are ok. I am here to tell you that this is the wrong attitude. Tenants don't want their rent increased so often they don't tell owners of maintenance items.

When I bought my business I instituted an annual preventative maintenance program and the first year it was implemented I had three apartments that had no p-traps (plumbing pipes) under the bathroom sink. Tenants had put buckets under the sink and when full emptied into the tub! We did the repair and had to convince and educate the tenants that since they pay rent, they deserve to have items in the home work. It is their responsibility to report maintenance items. We had to reassure them that we weren't going to raise their rent to cover the cost of the maintenance. So, just because you hear nothing from tenants don't assume everything is ok. In the long run, it could cost you a ton of money. In the past I have had to completely gut bathrooms because of a tiny water drip that was never reported. Do inspections, and have a maintenance management program that both you and the tenant agree to follow.

Relationships

Stay in touch with tenants, build and maintain a good relationship with tenants, and your vendors. When emergencies arise you need your vendors to step up and help out and they will go the extra mile if you keep in touch with them.

Through my business I hold contests to reward tenants. Some of them have been:

- Pay rent by the 1st of the month and get entered in a drawing for a gift card to a local business such as a favorite local restaurant.
- If you have had a great experience with our company give us a review and we'll send a little thank you gift card (Starbucks, gas card, Baskin Robbins) in the mail.
- When our maintenance staff does work at a property they leave a survey card behind – send in the card get entered into a drawing for a gift card. When a tenant has a baby or gets married we send congrats cards and we will post photos of the happy event to our company Facebook page and website.

With my personal rentals for Thanksgiving I send a Thank You for Being My Tenant card along with a gift card for a free pie. One year I forgot and just sent $20 to each tenant. I got a card back saying, "I hadn't had money fall from a card since I was a kid... What a great surprise and how fun!"

With my vendors I have done the following:

- Ordered and had delivered to my plumber's office pizza for the entire staff and crew. Did the same for my CPA around tax time – they loved it and appreciated the thoughtfulness.
- I have sent flowers to vendors,
- I have given gas cards to contractors and gardeners
- I have even sent a singing telegram to a few of my vendors. They even posted the event on their Facebook page.

As mentioned before I do an annual Client Appreciation event where I invite both owners and vendors. Owners love meeting the vendors who are doing work on their rentals and will often use them for their personal property. One year I took a bunch of photos and made coffee cups with the photos for my clients. My favorite coffee cup that I made is a client that lost his wife ten years ago. He always visits our office with his little dog Chloe and all his emails to us are signed Bob and Chloe. I made a cup for him with a picture of himself holding Chloe, which he always mentions when he sees us.

During the holiday season I make a donation to a local charity on behalf of my owners, which I match as a company. I let the owner's know in their monthly accounting statement what charity we chose. I started doing this because not all of my clients live locally so they tend to miss out on some of the client events. But this way they are able to be part of the community and really appreciate that we have included them.

It doesn't have to cost much but show appreciation to your tenants and vendors. It will go a long way in building the relationship.

Remember- managing rentals is a business and any part of running a business is management.

N

Notices – 3-day, 30-day, 60-day, 90-day, 24-hour; Change of Terms of Tenancy

Notices

People often get confused over the variety of notices and when to use which ones. I will outline the ones mentioned above. I am not an attorney, but these are the notices we tend to use in our business. If you have a chronic problem with a tenant just go straight to a landlord/tenant attorney or an eviction attorney to make sure you are doing things correctly.

When posting notices such as the 3-day or 24-hour notices you will want to post them on the door for the world to see. Make sure to take a photo of the posting in case you end up in court. For the 30, 60, and 90-day notices we always mail with a certificate of mailing so we have a date stamp of when the notice went in the mail. If we have a problematic tenant, we will post the notice on front door, mail, and scan it into an email so the tenant can't say they didn't receive the notice. We then follow up with a phone call a week later to make sure they got the notice.

3-Day to Pay Rent or Quit

This notice is used if you haven't received the rent by the due date. You post a 3-day notice to pay rent or move out. For the notice to be legal in California, you need to tape it to the door so it is visible by everyone. In my office we also take a photo of the notice posted on the door with a date on the picture in case we end up in court. I have won cases because of this step. We had a tenant tell the judge I taped an envelope to the door with a notice inside, but I had the photo that proved we posted the actual notice to the door. Be aware that in the notice you can only ask for the rent owed, you cannot add a late or bounced check fee. If at the end of 3 business days the rent still isn't paid then you proceed to eviction.

3-Day to Perform or Quit

This notice is posted (on the door for the world to see) if the tenant has violated the terms of the lease, for example a noise complaint or they have a pet and the lease says no pets. You post a 3-day notice for them to correct the situation, such as get rid of the pet, or they have to move.

30-Day Notice to Vacate

You can give this to your tenant if they are on a month-to-month rental contract or if their lease lasts less than a year. Hint: always make your lease just short of a year. For example, if the lease date is March 1st then make sure that the lease expires February 28th. You do not need to give reason for giving notice.

Tenants only need to give a 30-day notice to an owner. You'll want to put that you want a written 30-day notice in the lease or the month-to-month contract so that a tenant doesn't show up on the last day of the lease with keys in hand.

60-Day Notice to Vacate

This notice is given if tenant has lived in the property for more than 12 months. The only exception here is if the tenant that has been in the property for 12 months or more has a roommate move in who has been there less than 12 months. Then you can give a 30-day notice to both tenants. Again, you do not need to give a reason for the notice.

90-Day Notice to Vacate

If you participate in the Section 8 housing voucher program you need to give 90-day notice because it takes a tenant longer to find another owner who participates in the program. You also need to send a copy of the notice to the Housing Authority so they are aware and will stop payments to the landlord at the end of the 90-day notice. Section 8 is a housing subsidy program through HUD (Housing and Urban Development). This is a federal agency.

24-Hour Notice

This is used anytime you, the owner, wants to come to the property for an inspection or maintenance. You need to give the tenant a 24-hour notice that you will be at the property. You can mail the notice or you can post the notice on the door if you aren't able to reach the tenant by phone. This notice is required even if you will only be outside. For example, if you need to replace a fence and you need to go to property to take a look at it you still need to give 24-hour notice.

This notice is the one that most landlords don't provide and as a result wonder why a tenant gets upset when they arrive and knock on the door. Most landlords are shocked when they discover they need to provide notice to step onto the property. They somehow assume because they are outside of the home no notice is required. This is wrong. Always provide a notice. If you get verbal agreement from the tenant then just send an email confirming they are ok with the time both of you have arranged for the visit.

Change of Terms of Tenancy

The Change of Terms of Tenancy Form is used anytime you want to make changes to the rental agreement. Keep in mind if you have a lease you must wait until the lease term has ended before you can make any changes. If the tenant is on a month to month you can make changes anytime you want with the use of the Change of Terms of Tenancy Form. You need to send this form at least 30 days before any change can take effect.

Here are some examples of when you would use this form:
- Rent increase
- Deposit increase
- Adding a pet to the rental agreement
- Adding/removing residents to the lease
- Extending the lease for another year
- Providing access to laundry facilities

Basically, if you are going to change anything to the original lease this is the form that would be used.

O

Organization & Operations

Organization

Even if you have only one rental you need to be organized and have a system that keeps all your records in order. I have a binder with the following tabs and contents:

- Summary- Includes a sheet with tenant contact info, rental amount, security deposit amount, recent maintenance done
- Lease- Includes the lease and application, credit report, copy of move in, copy of move in money checks
- Maintenance- Includes the list of recent and future maintenance for the property
- Budget- Includes the checkbook, bank statements, property taxes, insurance, mortgage statements
- Communication- Includes the phone log of conversations, letters sent and received

If you have more than one property you definitely need a system. If you aren't good at accounting then you might want to consider hiring a local bookkeeper to help. Your CPA will appreciate you being organized especially when it comes to doing the taxes for your rental. In the long run you will save a lot of money.

Being organized helps you not only to assess when to raise rents, but to review the last maintenance work that was done. So when a tenant calls and reports a toilet backup in the hall bathroom you can see if the plumber has already been to the property five times this year. If so, you can assess why, maybe the roots are getting into the pipes and you need to set aside money for a potential line replacement, which is very expensive, and you don't want to be surprised by this emergency expense. I just had five properties at my rental company recently that had to have lines replaced at a cost of $10,000-$25,000 per line!

In my business we also keep information for each property in 5 section folders with the following tabs:

- Property Info which includes a copy of the original ad posting, assessor info, and property details such as "house," "2 bed/1 bath," "2 car garage," etc.
- Invoices for any maintenance done on the property
- Communication which includes tenant and owner emails
- Owner Info which includes insurance, taxes, and the management contract
- Tenant Info which includes lease, addendums, notices, and any rent increases
- If I have an Owner with many properties I have a separate Owner file that contains info that would apply to all the properties.

Whatever system you decide to use, set one up and use it. Please don't have a shoe box or drawer that you just toss everything into and then try to sort at tax time. This isn't treating your rental as a business.

Operations

You should have organizational systems, or at minimum, checklists for everything. Remember, even if you own just one rental, you need to treat it as a business. In your rental business you must account for the following:

- HR for tenant/vendor relationships
- Marketing for advertising, pictures, and applications
- Leasing for screening applicants, showing properties, processing and approving applications, creating leases, tenant lease signings, and collecting money
- Maintenance for handling move out, prepping for move in, cleaning, and handling any potential maintenance issues when a tenant has moved in
- Accounting for receiving move in funds and rent, returning deposits, paying maintenance bills and property bills such as insurance, taxes, and mortgages
- Administration for insurance renewal, refinancing, letters to tenants, posting notices, handling security deposit returns, and anything else that is administrative)

You need to have procedures in place for how you do these things in order to run a successful business. By having your Operations in order you won't be putting out fires all the time.

P

Personality Characteristics, Patience, Preventative Maintenance, Pets, Policies & Procedures, Photos, Profit

Personality Characteristics

Do you have the personality to be a landlord? Everyone thinks it is easy– just collect the rent. Well, if you have ever been a landlord you know that there is a lot more to collecting rent and sometimes that isn't so easy either. So what traits do you need to be a good landlord? Take the quiz and find out!

How Ready Are You To Be A Landlord?

Be honest with yourself about your skills and experience.
Mark your answers on a scale of 1-10:
1= Absolutely no   5 = Neutral   10 = Absolutely yes

1. Are you a person who enjoys working with others?
2. Are you able to keep your emotions in check and out of any business decisions?

3. Are you a patient and reasonably tolerant person?
4. Do you have the temperament to handle problems, respond to complaints, and service requests in a positive and rational manner?
5. Are you well organized in your daily routine?
6. Do you have strong time management skills?
7. Are you meticulous with your paperwork?
8. Do you have basic accounting skills?
9. Are you a good negotiator?
10. Are you willing to commit the time and effort required to determine the right rent for your rental unit?
11. Are you familiar with or willing to find out about the laws affecting property management in your area?
12. Are you willing to consistently and fairly enforce all the property rules and rental policies?
13. Are you interested in finding our more about property management?
14. Are you willing to learn new interpersonal skills?
15. Are you willing to make the commitment to learning about being your own property manager?

TOTAL POINTS:

So how did you do? What are your strengths and what are your weaknesses? The higher the score the better you will do being a landlord.

If you are a softie (which isn't bad!) but would describe yourself as a person who lives with your heart on your sleeve then you need to hire a good property manager. Every potential tenant that you would want to stay far away from will seek you out and will take advantage of you because you are caring, and want to help people.

I think being organized, professional and being able to say no are very important to a landlord's success. If you are weak in accounting then hire a part time bookkeeper. Do what you do best and get help with your areas of weakness or as mentioned before hire a professional property manager.

So that leads to the question how do I find a good property manager? This is where I believe that the characteristics for being an excellent property manager are different than the characteristics for being an excellent real estate agent who does sales. In property management you need someone who is: patient, knows the law, loves details, is organized, likes being in a relationship with someone day in and day out for years, is an excellent listener and facilitator, and has the ability to say NO to enforce the rental agreement.

In sales the relationship is a shorter duration. Successful agents are excellent sales people. They are great with people but usually have very little interest in the paperwork side of things. From my experience real estate agents find the routine of property management mundane and boring. Agents get great satisfaction from getting the listing and selling it and moving on to the next deal.

My advice is to find a professional property manager with years of experience who doesn't do sales. They might work in a real estate office but they are a dedicated property manager. When the sales market crashed and the sales agents livelihoods dried up some turned to property management and when the market recovers they will go back to sales. The biggest disadvantage to the owner is the liability that is created because the sales agent doesn't know all the laws and intricacies of property management. They are experts at sales, not property management.

My advice for anything is to go with the expert in the field. No one person can do everything perfectly.

Patience

Always outline in detail what you want done with the property and in the lease. When tenants ask what seems to be stupid questions be patient and happy that they are asking you first. Educate your tenant.

Preventative Maintenance

It's important to annually replace batteries in smoke detectors, check for drips, change filter in heater, and do a visual check of the roof, gutters, outside and inside. Look for health and safety issues such a potential trip hazard, evidence of rodents, that all doors and windows lock, and outside lights work. A checklist that can be used annually will be very helpful. Once you have a few years under your belt with your property you will be able to see if there are trends and things you need to set aside money for such as replacing gutters, screens, roof, water heater, major plumbing, heating/AC etc. Handling maintenance on a preventative basis will save you costly repairs down the road.

Pets

There are good, responsible, tenants who own pets. Personally I like pet owners and most have been wonderful with no damage to the property. Santa Cruz is a very pet friendly community and we were running into tenants who had pets and owners who wouldn't accept them. The fear owners have is the pets will destroy the property. So in order to open more of our properties to accepting pets, we started a pet program. This program has been a huge success for everyone involved. The property owner gets a higher rent in exchange for allowing a pet and reassurance through our inspections twice a year; tenants are so happy and appreciative to have a home that allows pets, who in reality are family to the tenant; and for us as a company because we are able to rent out our properties quickly to wonderful people.

How our program works is:

- Applicants must bring in the pet for us to meet and evaluate their overall behavior.
- Pets have to be approved by us prior to being approved for the property.
- Once approved for the property we take photos of the pets, get their names and interests and post to our company website's Pet Page.
- As part of our lease we add an emergency form for the

Veterinarian, a pet addendum, and renter's insurance.

- At the lease signing we collect the move in monies, which include an extra amount for the pet that is applied to the total deposit.
- We schedule two inspections and the tenants pay us to go do the inspection. Owners love this since they don't have to pay for it. Tenants are more than happy to pay for us to inspect the property.
- We send photos and a brief summary of the inspection to the property owner.

Keep in mind that a therapy or comfort animal is NOT considered a pet. Therefore you cannot charge a pet deposit or increase the rent to accommodate for the animal. You also cannot deny an applicant because of their therapy or comfort animal. I will address this more in the T section, under Therapy (Comfort) Animals.

That being said, here is the best way to ensure success if you do want to open your property to be pet friendly:

- Remember to check with your insurance carrier; some pets are not allowed by the insurance company.
- Put in your advertisement that pets are negotiable, you collect an extra amount towards the deposit, and that the tenant must participate in two annual inspections of the property.
- Meet the pet before you approve the applicant, and take photo of pet for your files. Remember to ask for the vet and emergency contact for the pet in case owners are not home and something happens.
- When preparing the lease have a pet addendum outlining what damage is not considered wear and tear. You also want to require the tenant to have Renter's Insurance, which would cover pet damage as well.
- At lease signing when you collect the money make sure to collect the extra amount for the pet. This extra amount gets added to the entire deposit. Do not call it a pet deposit. Remember, the extra amount added to the deposit can't cause the deposit to exceed 2 times the total rent. I do not recommend people charge an extra amount monthly and call it pet rent. What if the pet no longer is at the property and now tenant asks to have the rent lowered?
- Be sure to take photos of the property before the tenant moves in.
- Remember to do two annual inspections.

Policies & Procedures

Make sure your tenants know and understand what policies and procedures you have before they move in. Stick to your policies. If you have policies already in place then you will know how to answer when the tenant asks if they can store their RV in the driveway, if they can paint the walls with their favorite colors, or if they can pay rent on the 7th of each month when your lease states the 1st and late after the 5th. By having policies and procedures I can always say, "I am so sorry but our policy is..." I am confident, not wishy-washy. The few times I have made an exception to my policies and procedures it has come back to bite me. The perfect example is when the rent hasn't arrived by the due date and the tenant tells you the check is in the mail, and now it is the 15th of the month and you still haven't received the rent. The policy you have is the rent is due the 1st and late the 5th that means you should post the 3-day notice to pay or quit on the 6th. If the tenant pays on the 6th great, you have covered your bases. The tenant will also know you stick to your policies and won't play any games with them. Remember the lease is a legal contract so you need to enforce the contract when it is being violated. You think you are doing someone a favor by accepting rent late for example but it can come back to haunt you. Stick to your procedures.

Photos

Take photos of the unit before the tenant moves in, during inspections, and at move out. Make sure the pictures have the date imprinted. This will be important if you ever go to court, remember, a picture is worth a 1,000 words. I always take photos. I use them for advertising to rent the unit and I use them at the time I return the security deposit. If there are any discrepancies I print the photos and include them with the security deposit check so the tenant can see why I held back money for cleaning the toilet. If you ever go to court the judge will ask if you have photos. Once you take photos/videos and encourage tenants to take photos at move in as well you will no longer hear the common tenant mantra, "I left this place cleaner than when I moved in." Photos for advertisements should show the property in a good light. I have seen some horrific photos posted on rental sites. Please flush the toilet and put the seat down, please pick up the clothes off the floor. If the property is so messy you can't take photos to advertise then you probably shouldn't show the unit until the tenant has vacated. It will only turn potential applicants off to the property.

Profit

I am always saying treat your rental as a business. You should be aiming to make a profit at some point - in 5 years or 10 years or as a tax write off. Know your goal for holding the real estate. Rents should be slightly below market but raise the rent annually at least a little bit. You are not in the position to be subsidizing someone else's life style. It is a business arrangement.

Q

Question, Qualifying an Applicant, Quality – Product & Service

Question

As the owner you should always ask a lot of questions. When screening applicants, ask questions but make sure they are legally ok to ask. I would recommend that you take a Fair Housing Class so you are aware of what you can ask and what you can't ask. A good rule of thumb is to ask the questions that are on a rental application. Ask open-ended factual questions such as, "Why are you moving?" "How much is your income?" "How many occupants 18 years and older will be applying?" You cannot ask any questions that would be categorized as discriminatory such as, "Are you married?" "Do you have children?" "How many children?" "What nationality is your last name?"

Once you have a tenant keep the relationship professional and open. You want tenants to trust you to call when they have questions. One way to elicit questions is to be a good listener and to ask thoughtful questions of the tenant that show you are listening to them. When you get a maintenance emergency call, ask questions to understand the situation. Maybe you can walk tenant through a solution but if not, then you will know what type of vendor to call and whether it needs to be taken care of right away. Question your insurance agent annually to make sure your investment is properly insured. Be proactive in staying on top of laws and maintaining your relationship with your tenant. Don't be afraid to ask your tenant how things are going with the unit. By asking questions in a caring way you allow your tenant to feel comfortable coming to you when issues arise. Questioning allows you to stay informed and educated about being a landlord. Be open to questions and ask a lot of them.

Qualifying an Applicant

You want to know what your criteria for renting will be ahead of time. How much income compared to rent do they have to make? How long is their employment history, rental history? You want to ask all the same questions you would find on an application over the phone to pre-qualify them. Ask their credit score, how much income do they make, why are they moving, what is their job and how long have they been in it? Many times you can screen someone out over the phone thus saving you time showing the property. The way I position my phone screening is that I want to make sure I am not wasting their time since I am sure they are looking at many, many, potential rentals. Applicants are always appreciative when you are honest with them but always be willing to show the property if they are still interested in seeing it after doing a drive-by. Keep in mind in order to abide by Fair Housing Laws you CANNOT ask questions about family, children, sexual orientation, race, or nationality. I ask, "How many people are in your party?" or "How many occupants will be living in the unit?"

Ask questions and listen to how they are answered, the tone, the attitude etc. Are the answers vague? If so ask for more detail. Ask them what they are looking for in a unit and be quiet. Know your criteria and stick to it. If you apply the same criteria to everyone then you aren't discriminating and you will be more confident when questions are asked of you. I include my two-page criteria form with my application. I give everyone the entire packet so everyone knows the criteria so they can determine for themselves if they fit or not. For example, do you accept people who have a bankruptcy that isn't discharged? Do you accept someone with debt that is larger than $1,000? If someone is self-employed what financial information do you want to see to help qualify him or her?

Again, bottom line, have your criteria in place and ask lots of questions over the phone before you even show the property. Once you get the filled out application you MUST check everything on the application to verify that it is accurate. Good applicants rise to the top quickly both from paperwork you collect and from referrals of past landlords and employers.

If you are getting a ton of calls on the property you will be spending all day and night screening people. In this situation just let applicants know what the showing time is and they are welcome to come. If the unit is still occupied by a tenant limit the number of people you will show the property to. You will want to escort people through the unit a few at a time. If the property is vacant you can show it to as many people at one time as you like. Just have everyone arrive at your scheduled time and you can answer questions then. Don't stay at property for more than 30 minutes if you have a lot of people. They can see it, take an application, and get it to you if interested. Usually the person with the worst credit or rental history will be the one asking a ton of questions and sharing their life story with you. They are trying to form a relationship with you so that you will overlook their bad credit, eviction, whatever the situation is that is making it difficult for them to find housing. Keep to your policies and procedures. The showing time you have set is all the time you are going to remain at the property.

Quality — Product & Service

In business you want to provide a quality product (the rental) and quality service (how you manage the rental). Ideally, never show a property unless it is vacant and ready for move in. However, if your current tenant is neat and clean and their furnishings actually make the place look better than if it was vacant then go ahead and show the property. If unit is dirty or messy then it's better to wait until it is vacant. If you have a quality product (clean, fresh, functional, safe) then you can charge more money.

The service you provide is your professionalism in screening, having your paperwork in place, knowing your policies and being able to confidently answer any questions you get, doing maintenance when needed, being respectful of tenant time when scheduling inspections and giving 24 hour notice for being on property. Professional and respectful communication during and through the move out is crucial to a successful rental experience.

If you have both you will have a successful business. Your tenant will refer their friends to rent from you because they had such a wonderful experience.

R

Reserves, Roommates, Relatives, Rental Rate, Red Flags, Relationship

Reserves

Reserves are very important for investors, and property owners. You never know when the roof will leak, the water heater will go out or some other unexpected maintenance item will pop up. I keep saying this again and again but you need to treat your rentals as a business and you need to protect your business and investment by having reserves to cover unexpected expenses, including no rent for an extended period of time. I like to have between 5,000 and 10,000 in reserves. If you are in positive cash flow then maybe at minimum a couple thousand since you will get rents to cover the rest. In my business all properties must have $500 in reserves at all times to cover maintenance costs that come up after we have given owners their money for the month. Your reserves should include the tenant security deposit, a couple months of unpaid rent, taxes, insurance, and ideally a couple thousand to cover higher expenses that may pop up. Even if you put this on a credit card you will still need to pay the bill when it is due. By having reserves you immediately lower your stress level when something unexpected does happen.

Roommates

If you rent to roommates you want to make sure that each qualifies and passes your screening test independently of the other. The monthly rent check should be one check collected by you, not individual checks. You rent a house not rooms in a house. Make one roommate the point person that you will communicate with regarding the property. You want to list all roommates on the lease. If they are students, you will want to get a parent to co-sign the lease. This guarantees that they guarantee the rent and make sure they are aware that they are responsible for all roommates, not just their child, in the case of late rent or damages. This often will cause parents to think twice about co-signing and it should.

Relatives

My one piece of advice that I always dispense at classes or workshops and I will share with you now is – Never Rent To Relatives – NEVER. If they don't pay rent are you really going to evict them? Friends and Family comingling with your rental business is never going to end well. Just don't do it. If little Johnny needs a place to live then co-sign on an apartment for him and if he doesn't pay rent then he hasn't become your problem. You'll cover the rent as co-signer and work with landlord to move Johnny out of the apartment.

Rental Rate

How do you determine the fair market value of your property? Look in the papers (yes, some markets still use the classifieds section of the newspaper). I have a personal rental in an area where people just don't use Craigslist and I have to pay to list in the paper. I hate it but that is the local market. Look on Craigslist or other online rental websites to see what comparable properties are renting for but please keep in mind many of these online sites often aren't accurate. The best place to look for accurate rental rates are on the websites of local property management companies. Property managers have their finger on the pulse of the community and they aren't going to keep a property on their listing page for months. I often get called to visit a property to give a fair market rent price on the rental. I have often thought about charging for my visits but I never have. I can always tell when someone really doesn't want my service they just want me to price it for them so they can advertise and rent it themselves. It gives me an opportunity to educate the person and maybe in the future they will think of me if they do need property management services.

Price the property slightly below the market average. Put your advertisement out there and you should start getting calls immediately, if not then drop the price aggressively not by $10 or $20 but by $50-$100. If the market is hot and rental prices are increasing rapidly, set the price at the high-end but be prepared to drop it by as much as $200 increments if you aren't getting any takers. You want to get lots of calls so you get lots of applications and lots of good prospects. The longer your property sits on the market the less traffic you will get and the more money you lose. You can't make up one month of lost rent. If you don't want to drop rent, drop the security deposit, open the property to pets or offer a move-in incentive.

Red Flags

Here are my top red flags of things to watch out for when showing a property:

1. The applicant can move in now and tries to rush you.
2. The applicant wants to pay with cash or personal check for their move in funds at the lease signing. (More on this later in the section.)
3. The applicant offers to pay rent for 6 months to a year in advance.
4. The applicant talks fast and doesn't allow you to ask questions.
5. The applicant's story changes.
6. Different people other than the applicant show up at the showing.
7. The applicant talks too much; they tell you their life history, sad story, etc.
8. The applicant's supporting documentation gets complicated/their story gets complicated
9. They don't have credit, references, job, or rental history – I have experienced this, really.
10. They are vague and get upset with the screening questions
11. The applicant doesn't follow your instructions; so will they follow the lease?
12. The application is left blank

13. The applicant says they have a Labrador but in fact it is a Pit Bull. Always meet the pet if you are going to accept one – a Lab mix is not the same as a Pit Bull

NEVER accept a personal check for move in funds (rent, security deposit, pet deposit). It's ok to accept one for the monthly rent but not the initial move in funds. I heard a story from a property manager that had a well-known property developer in the area sitting at their doorstep ready to move in immediately and wanted to pay with a personal check. Because of this person's excellent reputation and the fact that the moving van was ready to unload, the property manager felt pressured and rented to him. Well, he moved in, the check bounced and then the property manager had to evict him. He also filed for bankruptcy, which halted the eviction. So learn from someone else's mistake and don't ever feel pressured to accept anything less than guaranteed funds.

Another big red flag is when someone tells you their life story; are you prepared to get more stories like this monthly when the rent isn't paid on time? Another thing that can get overlooked is holes in their application. Where were they living for 6 months? I once had an applicant that I asked where she had been living for 18 months since there was a blank period of time and she said she was in the county jail. At least she was honest.

At times you will have a prospect ask if you will take less rent and sometimes that is followed by an offer to exchange services for lower rent such as, "I will do the gardening," or "I am a contractor and can do the maintenance if you will consider less rent." My standard statement is, "We don't negotiate during showings. Apply and if you are a strong applicant we can discuss the possibility," only if you want to consider lower rent. My feeling is why is someone looking at a property for $2700 and only wants to pay $2000? They should be looking at $2000 priced properties. For professionals such as landscapers who will usually ask for lower rent to do the landscaping my standard response is, "Give me a bid to do the yard and if it is reasonable we will pay you to do the yard but we won't reduce the rent." They always say, "Well I don't want to do that." I then let them know they can now come home at the end of a long day and have a wonderful yard that they don't have to work on but can enjoy.

Relationships

Start the tenant/landlord relationship in a positive way. Always come from a place of positive intent instead of assuming the tenant is out to screw you. Try to put yourself in their shoes. Always be professional, respectful, and try to find solutions.

Listen and document. You aren't their best friend; you are their landlord so keep the relationship defined. It keeps the boundaries clear. Be friendly and approachable so tenants will want to report maintenance issues and never be accusatory even if you are right. You always want a win/win even if that means you help move the person along. When people are pushing my buttons, I stop, and my approach is to kill them with kindness.

S

Security Deposits, Screening Applicants, Showings, Small Claims Court, Systems

Security Deposits

Security Deposits are always tricky. I was just speaking with a landlord yesterday that was having a problem with a tenant they rent to and I asked how much was the security deposit - there was none! I also recently picked up a 4-plex to rent and 1 of the units had never paid a security deposit. California law states you can collect 2 times the rent for an unfurnished property and 3 times the rent for a furnished property. In my business our standard is 1.5 times the rent. If you accept pets you will want to collect extra towards the total security deposit but you cannot exceed the 2 times rent for the deposit including the extra charge for pet. Don't call the money for the pet a "pet deposit" because that is all you will have available to you in the event of damages. If you put the extra amount for the pet toward the total deposit then you have the total deposit available to you if there are damages.

If there are roommates and one moves out I do not get involved in a partial return of security deposits. I rent a house not rooms. I only return the total deposit when everyone moves out. Remaining roommates are responsible for the partial disposition of deposits.

When you do a rent increase remember to also increase the deposit so it stays in line with the rent. There's nothing like having a tenant for 10 years and their rent is now $2,000 and the deposit is $900 and they move out without paying last month rent. You end up without enough deposit to cover the unpaid rent let alone any possible damages.

It is illegal to collect first, last and deposit in some States. According to California law you can't accept more than 2 times the rent for an unfurnished unit for deposit plus rent so that kind of eliminates the first, last and deposit. Insider's tip, it is never a good idea to accept last month's rent. Why? What if your tenant gives you notice to move after 10 years and you have raised the rent over the years so now the current rent is $2,000 but at the time of move in it was only $1,000 well now you will be short changed your last month's rent and legally you can't ask for the difference or take it from the deposit.

We collect rent and deposit. We never make the deposit the same amount as rent because the tenant will think they paid last month rent when it comes time for them to move. Even in my business it isn't uncommon for tenants to give us a 30-day notice and not pay rent. When we contact them they say, "We paid last month at move in." We have to show them their lease stating they paid rent and deposit. Now they panic because they don't have money for rent because they used that money to put down on the new rental. If this happens work with tenant to make sure the house is clean and you can give them a full refund minus the last month rent you held back. This is another reason to not have the deposit equal the rent. What if there are damages? You want to manage risk.

Screening Applicants

Do your due diligence and verify everything on the rental application, including an applicant's prior landlord, not just current one. Do the same with their employers. Check credit, pay stubs, bank accounts– everything. When screening ask lots of questions, particularly open-ended questions such as: "How do you know this person?" If the applicant is vague keep probing. It doesn't mean they are lying, they just aren't telling you everything so ask and listen. I have seen tenants that keep things close to the vest and won't tell you that their true intent is to move in their boyfriend after they get the unit or that they have a pet and don't disclose it, so you have to ask lots of questions to uncover things. If they are vague you may not want to have them as a tenant because they are hiding things. Listen closely to answers from the references. What are they not saying?

If your applicant is a student who doesn't have credit or much in the way of references, ask to see school transcripts. What is their

GPA (grade point average)? Are they a good student or not? Ask for teachers or coaches as references. Ask for a resume. Speak with their parents to find out if they paid rent while at home, etc. If the applicant is a retiree who often pays with cash, ask to see their bank accounts and social security benefits. Bottom-line, you have to spend time checking all the information that is on the application or getting more supporting information to satisfy that they will be responsible paying tenants.

In my ten plus years as a professional I have seen three falsified tax returns. I have seen false pay stubs and of course, false landlord references. So double check all information and ask good follow up questions.

Showings

Screen potential applicants over the phone first, and ask if they did a drive-by and viewed photos online. Once you have screened over the phone set a time for a showing. You set the time, don't let them jerk you all over the place. If they are serious they will make the time you set. I got tired of no shows and hours of wasted time waiting. So, now I tell everyone THEY need to call 1 hour prior to the showing to RECONFIRM that they will be at the property otherwise I don't show up. This has worked really well for me.

The one exception is if the phone is ringing off the hook. If you answer it every time you will spend all day and night screening people. So just set a time, about 30 minutes, to show the property and mention the date and time on your answering machine so you don't even have to answer the phone. Be at the property and answer questions there. We do this in the summer when it is our busy season. We also often put the showing date and time in our online advertisement and just let people show up. We have lots of applications, answer all questions in front of the crowd, and we only stay 30 minutes. Only the serious people will apply and you have only spent about an hour of your time.

For safety reasons never do a showing when it is dark outside. Never go into the property with the person behind you. Get to the property early, turn on the lights, open the blinds and wait for the person inside. If the property is remote never show alone, always take someone with you. I don't do open houses. I show a property for 15-20 minutes by appointment only. That is all the time that is necessary for someone to decide if they want to apply. If the possible applicant asks right off the bat if I will take less money for the property- I always say NO. They need to apply, and if they are a strong applicant I might consider it.

It's better to say that you are the property manager; don't say you are the owner. When I show properties I never say I am the owner of the business. I don't even say I am the property manager, I have my name badge and that is it. For all they know I am the receptionist. This allows me to observe their behavior such as do they take their shoes off before entering the house, or do the kids run screaming through the house slamming doors while the parents are oblivious?

Small Claims Court

I addressed this information in C under Court. Hopefully you will never end up here. Do your due diligence, follow your systems, policies and procedures and you will most likely be able to avoid going to Small Claims Court. The majority of property owners that end up here are because they didn't handle the security deposit return properly. They either kept all the money and didn't document it properly and/or they didn't get the deposit returned within the legally required number of days. Know the law and you can avoid some of these costly mistakes.

Systems

I have talked about this before in section O under Organization and P under Policies & Procedures. You want to have your procedures and systems in place, including your filing system, banking system, maintenance system, and tenant communication system. If you have a system in place then when things come up you know how to handle them without getting stressed or agitated with the tenant.

T

Taxes, Turnovers, Time Management, Trust, Therapy/Comfort Animals

Taxes

Property taxes are due November 10th and February 10th but most owners pay by December 10th and April 10th. April taxes are tough because personal taxes are due as well. The most important thing to remember with taxes is to make sure to build up a money reserve monthly. When property values drop, as we have seen over the past few years, you can go to your county assessor's office and have your home revalued. If the value has dropped significantly you can get your property taxes lowered.

Turnovers

What is a turnover? It is the time when the property turns from one tenant over to another tenant. This is where you want to go in and do any maintenance that is necessary. This also might be the time to do a few cosmetic updates. I went into a property once to do a tenant placement for an owner who was going to manage her own unit and I was shocked it still had orange shag. I asked if the owner was going to replace the carpet and she said, "No, it still looks good." I was stunned. This same owner was what I would call a slumlord. The fridge still worked but was so rusty it was disgusting. Needless to say I didn't take the property to rent.

During turnovers is when you can do simple and very inexpensive updates. Change the electrical cover plates, put in new light fixtures ($20 at a home improvement store goes a long way). Take down drapes and put in blinds. Paint is really inexpensive; maybe fresh paint will brighten things up. Change out bathroom faucets to a more modern style- it doesn't have to be designer just something that doesn't look like it is straight from the 70s.

Clean up the yard if there is one, and make sure that the unit is sparkling clean when showing. I allow 5 days between tenant turnovers so as you can imagine I have all my vendors lined up to get in and out before the new tenant moves in or before we start advertising it.

Keep in mind that documentation and photos are your friends. Remember, you want to document the vacancy so you can accurately determine the deposit to be returned to the old tenant and to have new photos and notes in place for the new tenant. Again, have your system in place and this will make turnovers a lot easier.

Time Management

The saying, "Time is Money," is especially true with real estate and property management. Your time is valuable so plan it well.

Do your rental accounting monthly and put it on the calendar. Do your showings with groups of people all at once. Plan maintenance checks and do a couple things at one time. Have all your files organized so you don't spend time looking for things. Tax time will be a breeze if you are organized with your rentals, saving you tons of time, stress and money!

Trust

I am not an attorney but from my personal experience and in managing properties for 10 years I can't stress how important it is to set up a Living Revocable Trust. This is done through an estate attorney. People often have rental properties with the intent of leaving it to their kids but if a trust isn't set up it will go to probate. This means the property will end up in court after the owner passes away and it can take years to settle depending upon the size of the estate. Unfortunately in situations such as this much of the property might have to be sold in order to cover taxes and court and attorney fees.

This is exactly what happened to some ladies I know. Their dad had a very large real estate and property management company and I guess he thought he would live forever. He never set up a trust so when he passed, his daughters spent 8 years in court settling the estate. In the end they had to sell much of the estate to pay for all the fees. I am sure he didn't want his daughters to spend eight years in court and then have to sell the properties. So please, once you have a piece of real estate please seek out the advice of an estate planning attorney.

Therapy/Comfort Animals

It is illegal to deny an applicant solely because they have a therapy/comfort animal. This is true even if your building has a no pet policy. This gets back to Fair Housing Laws and discrimination based upon disability. You cannot ask why they need the animal. You cannot ask about their disability.

When I get someone that asks, "Do you take therapy/comfort animals?" we tell the person that they are welcome to apply and we will process them; if they meet our criteria they will be approved. There is no point in answering that question because it is a trap. You must take the animal if the person is approved so the first step is to have the person apply. If they don't qualify on income, credit, job history or your other criteria then they are denied based upon that information not because of the animal. If the applicant is approved you can ask for a doctor's letter indicating the animal is a comfort animal or if it's a therapy animal then you can ask for documentation of the certification for your file. You will want to make sure to document everything carefully.

What if a tenant has a Pit Bull as their comfort animal? Then you need to accept the animal. A comfort animal can be anything that brings comfort so that might be a snake, a bird, a dog, a cat, a fish, basically any animal. The animal owner needs to abide by the same animal addendum as anyone else. No excessive barking and no lunging or biting of people– the animal needs to be under owner control. If these things are violated then the tenant could be asked to move regardless if the animal is a therapy or comfort animal.

You cannot collect extra towards deposit or collect a pet rent. The animal isn't considered a pet. Bottom line, I don't think any of us would argue that a seeing-eye dog for a blind person isn't a good thing. You need to process the applicant like you would anyone else.

You will definitely want to do annual checks of the property to make sure it is in safe condition for the tenant and the animal and if there is damage caused by the animal the tenant is responsible.

U

Utilities, Unlawful Detainer, Underwater

Utilities

Utilities can be tricky if the tenant doesn't pay all the utilities themselves. Many multi-family properties have shared meters. The dilemma for property owners is if you include utilities in the rent, tenants tend to abuse them and leave the heater going 24/7– if they aren't seeing the bills they don't know the expense. I am a firm believer in tenants paying their utilities. There are a couple ways of doing this.

1. Prorate the utilities by number of occupants, or by square footage if one unit is very large and the other is small.
2. Owner pays up to a certain limit and anything over that the tenant pays.
3. Add second PGE (Pacific Gas & Electric) meter to other units and bill per the meter. You can do the same thing with water but it is extremely expensive to put in a separate water meter– I have looked into this several times and it doesn't make financial sense for me but check it out anyway.
4. I pay water for my tenants with their rent on my personal duplex but if the bill gets higher than normal I send a

copy of the bill to the tenants showing them the increase along with a letter asking for conservation or I will start charging and then they are good about it and the following bill is usually lower or back to the normal usage.

5. Some cities put all utilities on one bill including garbage. However, I have found that garbage, water and gas/electric are usually separately line itemed on the bill. If you want to include the water or gas/electric you can still charge for garbage service and this is usually easy to see and calculate. In my business we have many multi-family properties where tenants pay for their gas/electric and owner pays water (since it is one meter and we can't separate the bill out by tenant), but we do charge for the garbage, which is a separate charge on the total bill.

If you are going to include utilities with the rent make the rent high enough to cover the bill. This method works best for small studios or cottages- it doesn't work well for units of different sizes or duplexes.

When looking for investment properties to buy ask if the utilities are separately metered. Call the utility company to find out average bill for the year for the property and then you can add this to the entire aspect of facts as to whether you should buy the property or not.

Unlawful Detainer

This is the legal definition of Eviction. This has already been covered in the C section.

Underwater

This isn't referring to the house actually flooding. This means the mortgage on the property is higher than what the fair market value of the property is. In this situation there are 4 options:

1. Continue to pay mortgage if you can afford it.
2. Become a landlord by renting the property if you need to move for a job.
3. Short sell it. This is where the lender/bank takes less than the mortgage and you are able to sell it.
4. Foreclosure. This is where you walk away and the bank takes the house.

There is no perfect option. All of them have consequences. I would say option 1 is best if you can afford to pay the mortgage. If you need to relocate and still can afford the mortgage on the house then renting the house might work until values come up and you can sell. Short selling is a long process with a lot of stress because you have to get the bank to agree to take less money for the house. The last option will cause your credit score to plummet which will affect everything else you want to purchase. For example if you want a car the interest rate you will get will not be a good one because you will be seen as a bad credit risk. Although sometimes it is better to just walk away and start over. My best advice is to consult with your tax advisor for your personal situation.

V

Vendors & Vacancies

Vendors

Build strong relationships with vendors and have them in your phone contact list long before you need them. Always use the same vendor so you can build a relationship with them so they will come to your aid when you need them most. I am very good to my vendors. I give bonuses to them in December. In the slow months I make sure to pay them immediately not 30 days out. I also do an annual appreciation event, which is catered at a restaurant with rewards, certificates of appreciation, and gift certificates (gas cards are a real hit with vendors). I go see the work that the vendor has done (painting, carpet, vinyl, cleaning, etc.) and I give them kudos for a job well done. Keep in mind often these vendors are working in vacant units or meeting a very unhappy tenant so they don't get positive feedback or recognition. If you treat them right they will make your calls a priority. There is nothing worse than getting a call from your tenant that sewage is backing up and you are boarding a plane for Hawaii over the Christmas Holiday. Your vendor will come to your rescue if you have spent the time to build the relationship. Oh, and don't forget to bring back a thank you gift from Hawaii for your plumber.

Vacancies

Keep vacancies to a minimum. Advertise and show the property while the tenant is still in the unit - as long as it is clean. If the unit is really dirty or you need to do some real turnover cleaning then wait until tenant vacates - clean the unit and do what is needed to immediately start showing the property. Never show a property that isn't clean and ready to rent that day. Walls should be clean or freshly painted, the bathrooms and kitchen sparkling, carpets clean, windows clean, yard mowed etc. First impressions count.

List the rental price slightly below market value. You will get more qualified applicants than if you list for maximum value and have a 30-60 day vacancy. You can't make up the money you lose. I advertise a property and if I am not getting the calls I expect within 3 days I lower the price by $50-$100.00 immediately. Or, if the rent is a good price but the time of year is wrong (like November, December) then offer a discounted rent for the 6th and 12th month. The other option is to do a 6-month lease at a lower rent and then in summer increase the rent and offer a 1-year lease renewal to the tenant.

W

Wealth, Waste – Time & Money, Wear & Tear, Web

<u>Wealth</u>

Owning investment property is an excellent way to build long-term wealth. As long as you manage your property as an investment and business, your chances of building wealth will be good. Many people don't treat their rentals as an investment and therefore actually lose money. They don't maintain the property, the rent is too low, they pay for all utilities, they don't collect rent on time, etc. Investment properties cost money and it is worth having a good CPA on your side to advise you on what you can and cannot write off on your taxes. Investment properties are like any other part of your investment strategy; stocks, bonds, 401k etc. Real estate though is more hands on unless you have a management company handling everything. Building wealth takes work but has a huge payoff.

Waste – Time & Money

Again, manage your rental like a business so you don't waste your time. Have systems in place for managing showings, vacancies, and when maintenance gets done. Handle your accounting in a systematic way to save you time. Your time is worth something. Trying putting a dollar amount to an hour of your time. You might be shocked. All the time you spend at the property is costing you money. Don't be cheap with vendors - they save you time and yes, they cost money, but you can write all this off on taxes.

Did you know that as an owner you cannot write off your own time when you do a maintenance repair? You can write off the materials but not the time. So, why do it yourself? If you are doing a full remodel then ok, you will save a lot of money but if you have a plumbing repair– just call a plumber! I have one client that when a toilet needs to be switched out on the rental, he will go buy the toilet and then have the plumber install it. I am sorry but that is a waste of time and money! First, how long does it take to go find a toilet, purchase it and take it to the property? Then the plumber comes out and puts it in, but now there is no warranty for the toilet. You still have to pay the plumber their service charge so are you really saving anything?

The biggest piece of advice I can give property owners is to do an annual preventative maintenance check or have a contractor or handyman do it for you. We do this annually in the business and we find all kinds of little things that tenants always says to us, "It is small so I didn't want to bother you with it." Well, they are afraid of the rent increasing if they complain. The reality is that the small drip can eventually turn into something large and very expensive. It is also when I get to tell tenants to put the batteries back into the smoke detectors and if there is a fire they will be held liable. If the place looks like a dump then I let them know they have to clean it up because health and safety is at hand and their lease states the property has to be kept clean. These checks will allow you to save money and time in the long run. It will help determine if you want to renew the lease with the tenant, how many people are actually living in the residence and the overall care being taken with your investment.

I like the old saying, "A stitch in time saves nine." Please don't waste your valuable time and money micromanaging or ignoring your investment properties. Get help if you need it. On your death bed are you going to be saying, "I wish I had spent that Saturday snaking the plumbing at the rental."...God, I hope not, I hope you are thinking of how glad you are that you spent your free time with family, friends, and doing the things you love. What a better way to spend your time and money.

Wear & Tear

Wear and tear is hard to define but I am a common sense person and property manager. Here are some examples of what I consider normal wear and tear:

- The walls have some marks from furniture, a few nail holes
- Carpet might be frayed at front door entry
- A blind might have one slightly bent slat
- New vinyl might have a few scuff marks
- Kitchen counter might have a chip out of the tile or a scratch in the Formica

What is not considered normal wear and tear would be:

- A hole behind the door from the knob
- Crayon or pen painting on the kid's walls
- Holes of any kind in doors
- Large holes in walls for example from wall mounted TV's
- Stains in carpets
- Bent or broken slats in blinds
- Unit left dirty
- Newer appliances such as fridge with broken shelves or veggie bins
- Towel bars hanging from walls or missing altogether
- Water damage vinyl around toilet or tub
- Kitchen Formica counter with burn ring from hot pot being set on counter

"Wear and Tear" or "Damages?"

Normal "Wear & Tear" caused by ordinary comings and goings	"Damage" caused by carelessness, abuse, thievery, mysterious disappearance, accident, rules violation, or special request
Well-worn keys	Missing keys
"Sticky" key	Key broken off inside of lock
Difficult door lock	Door lock replaced by tenant without management's permission
De-pressurized fire extinguisher with unbroken seal	De-pressurized fire extinguisher with broken seal (not used to put out fire)
Worn pattern in plastic counter top	Burn in plastic counter top
Rust stain under sink faucet	Sink discolored by clothing or hair dye

Loose, inoperable faucet handle	Missing faucet handle
Discolored ceramic tile	Painted ceramic tile
Loose grout around ceramic tile	Chipped or cracked ceramic tile
Threadbare carpet in hallway	Rust marks on carpet from indoor plant container
Scuffing on wooden floor	Gouge in wooden floor
Linoleum with back showing through	Tear in linoleum
Wobbly toilet	Broken toilet tank lid
Rusty shower curtain rod	Kinked shower curtain rod
Rust stain under bathtub spout	Chip in bathtub enamel

Tracks on door jamb where door rubs	Hole in hollow core door
Door off its hinges and stored in garage	Missing door
Plant hanger left in ceiling	2 inch diameter hole in ceiling
Stain on ceiling caused by leaky roof	Stain on ceiling caused by popping champagne or beer bottles
Cracked paint	Crayon marks on wall
Chipped paint (minor)	Walls painted by tenant in dark color necessitating repainting
Pleasing, professional tenant wallpapering	Amateurish tenant wallpapering
Mildew around shower or tub	Mildew where tenant kept aquarium

Urine odor around toilet	Urine odor in carpet
Discolored light fixture globe	Missing light fixture globe
Odd-wattage light bulbs that work	Burned out or missing light bulbs
Light fixture installed by tenant which fits its location	Light fixture installed by tenant which must be replaced
Window cracked by settling or by high wind	Window cracked by movers
Faded shade	Torn shade
Paint blistered Venetian blinds	Venetian blinds with bent slats
Sun damaged drapes	Pet damaged drapes
Drapery rod which won't close properly	Drapery rod with missing parts

Dirty window screen	Missing bent or torn window screen
Ants inside after rainstorm	Fleas left behind by tenant's pet
Scrawny landscaping which was sparingly watered due to drought conditions	Neglected landscaping which must be replaced with similar plantings
Grease stains on parking space	Caked grease on parking space

Web

When advertising on Craigslist keep in mind you can't use words that discriminate such as "family home," "kids welcome," "perfect for seniors," etc. You can't say "No Section 8" either, but you can say, "Owner doesn't participate in the Housing Voucher Program (Section 8). You should post good photos that show the clean property.

Be very careful of scams. Delete any inquiry from someone out of the country wanting to rent sight unseen. My policy is you have to see the property before you can apply. Another scam is when people take your photos and description from Craigslist and change the advertisement and offer the same property for substantially less rent. You may get calls from people who are angry thinking you are trying to do a bait and switch. You can watermark the photos so it is harder to copy them. Google "watermarking photos" and you will find inexpensive downloadable software that can do this. This has made a huge difference in our office. We have our company website across all photos but you could put an email. Make sure to check on your property. I also recommend that you don't have any photos of the property address or list the address either, just mention the neighborhood or what well-known landmark it's near. This makes it more difficult for scammers to get your property and falsely advertise it. There have been situations where people send money ahead of time to the person impersonating the owner, meet the scam artist at the property and get a key from the scammer (who calls the locksmith and tells them they got locked out of their home) and come to find out the scammer runs off with the money and the owners find out the house is rented to someone they have never dealt with.

Use caution with people on the web. This is another reason to use a property management company for placement services. They have heard it all and know the scams.

X

Xerox & X-Check (Crosscheck)

Xerox

Copy documents and keep copies of all communication, whether on your computer or printed, and put into the property's file. The main point here is to document, document, and document. Have a filing system for your documents so you can find what you are looking for later. Copies can always be sent to the tenant and referenced in communication. If you are organized there is a less chance for you to get sued. Keep copies of all photos before and after move in, repairs, etc. Today with the speed of technology it is very easy to keep everything scanned online or in the cloud. There is no reason to not document everything.

X-Check (Crosscheck)

You'll want to cross check all references and everything on a tenant's application. Do your due diligence with referencing the web and books about property management so that you are educated and can answer and speak to any concerns or questions your tenants may have. Crosschecking your facts keeps your risk down from possible lawsuits. It is ok to not always have the answer. Just tell the tenant, "Let me check into your question and I will get back to you by..." and give a specific date. Otherwise, it will be viewed as a stall technique. Then make sure to get back to tenant with your answer and reference your information in case they want to check it out for themselves.

Y

Yearly Planning & Year-End Planning

<u>Yearly Planning</u>

Your yearly planning should be done before the New Year begins. It should also be reviewed quarterly. Again, this is your business and your investment. What should be part of your yearly planning?

- Any turnovers coming up, what maintenance needs to be done this year? Do you have a budget?
- Taxes, Insurance, Mortgage, Utilities - what are your fixed expenses and how much are they going to be?
- Have reserves in the bank. If you have a vacancy do you have the reserves set aside for turnover, and the return of the security deposit?
- Review insurance, and your mortgage to see if you need to make adjustments. You'd hate to find out after a fire that you didn't have enough insurance.
- Review the lease to see if there are any new legal addendums that need to be included with the lease, are there any changes to occupants - birth of a child, new roommate etc.?

- Compare your New Year budget with actual budget from prior year. Were you on track, over budget, under budget etc.?

Year-End Planning

Year-end planning is where you gather all your files, prepare for tax time, review the budget and see how you did. What changes were anticipated and unanticipated? This will help with the New Year planning. Set up new accounting spreadsheets, and a new file system for the coming year. I have set files, and I pull out all the documents in the files and put them in a large envelop with the property's address. Then I print my accounting spreadsheet for the entire year and staple it to the front of the envelope and give it to my accountant. I now have empty files and folders ready for the New Year. I go to my computer files and create new ones for the New Year.

This planning is vital and so important to do. If you just hate it, then hire a bookkeeper to do this for you. It is well worth the money to have someone organize this accounting. Remember this is your business. Get help where it is needed. Just like I don't expect all owners to be able to do plumbing, electrical or general contracting work, you shouldn't expect that you can do the accounting if it isn't your thing. You can write off the expense for taxes and this way you get all of your due write offs.

I can't stress the importance of doing your year-end and New Year planning. If you don't do this crucial part of property management then you might end up like my next and last topic of property management: Z for Zombie, where your energy is zapped and you lose your zest for life by being burdened with your rental property.

Z

Zero Sum Gain (Break Even), Zap Your Energy, Zombie, Zen, Zest for Life

Well I am on Z and covered all topics related to Property Management through the alphabet and then some. Hope you have found the topics timely and of interest.

Zero-Sum-Gain (Break Even)

Breaking even is at least where you want to be with your investment property and well on your way to positive cash flow. We all have negatives at some time with rental properties but it shouldn't be a long-term condition. Even with write-offs you don't want to be losing money indefinitely.

Zap Your Energy

Yes, property management can zap your energy. Even I have my days. However, if you have systems in place, follow the procedures you have set and keep on top of your accounting and maintenance, and work to build a good relationship with your tenant you should rarely be in a state of feeling Zapped or Zombie-like.

Zombie

You might feel like a zombie after doing a large turnover, or remodel. This isn't how you should feel managing your rental. You don't want to be in a place where you are going through the motions. If you are, then you aren't minding the store and treating the rental as a business, which if you have read this book you now know this is a constant theme with me. Your rental IS a Business. If you are feeling like a zombie- then hire a good property management company to take over for you.

Zen

This is where you want to be headed with your rentals. Yes, I live in Santa Cruz, CA and this term is probably better understood here than elsewhere. You want to be managing your properties in a way that it fits into your life, is a balanced part of your life, and shouldn't become your life because that is when people get fed up and just sell.

People forget their long-term goal for their investment and business and often just call it quits. Again, by following the tips and advice in this book you will be able to manage rental properties and hopefully have a balanced relationship with your rentals; getting you as close to Zen as possible.

Zest for Life

Remember when you inherited the property or bought your first rental? I do. I was so excited. It was my first big investment, my first step into diversifying my investments away from mutual funds by adding real estate into my portfolio; it was my first step towards my retirement planning. My first rental was also real, physical, something I could touch and actively participate in. I was so excited about remodeling, painting, making it mine and honoring my Dan's 96-year-old grandma who had lived in the home most of her life. The house became my first real estate purchase.

You want your rentals to be a part of an overall plan and something that should still get you excited about your goals and future. I still have a tangible sense of responsibility for taking care of my properties. I feel responsible to my tenants to provide a nice place to live. I feel responsible to myself to manage my investment well. My goal in buying my real estate was to keep it for the long-term and have them as part of my retirement plan. It was never to buy and flip.

In the past 20 years I have remodeled over 12 homes, and loved it. I got into property management because of my business background, organizational abilities, and exceptional communication skills. I finally listened to friends and family who kept saying, "Why don't you do property management as a business?" I took their advice, tested the field, and found I loved it. I have been blessed to be able to buy a 20 year old business from someone who was retiring and over the past 10 years I have been able to add my own touch to it, go out on my own, build my portfolio and staff, and create amazing relationships with my clients, tenants, vendors, employees and the community at large, along with finding a career that is challenging every day. I truly learn something new daily.

I have found my Zest in Life and love to share my experience and best business practices. I teach at Cabrillo Community College, and at other Real Estate related events.

Please check out my website at www.PortolaRentals.com, for relevant property management information, video blogs, tips and tricks. Please like us on Facebook where we post new topics, classes and workshops about property management. Join the conversation. I am always happy to answer questions and am available for consulting, coaching and speaking opportunities.

Index

Index

Annual Preventative Maintenance Checklist

Inspection Date: Time:
By:
Property Address:
Unit #
OK to Use Key #
OA Summary:
Photos:
Property Owner: Phone:
Tenants: Phone:
Was Tenant present?

	OK	Health Saftey	Needs Repair	N/A	Notes/ Action

A) Exterior
1) Front Yard/Entry

	OK	Health Saftey	Needs Repair	N/A	Notes/ Action
Fence/Gate					
Walks/Driveway					
Porch/Stairs					
Lighting					

Mailbox/House No's					
Exterior					
Other					

2) Backside/Yard

Patio/Deck					
Patio/Deck Cover					
Fence/Gate					
Lighting					
Exterior					
Other					

3) Landscaping

Sprinklers/Hose-bibs					
Shrubs/Trees					
Lawns/Cover					
Other					

4) Utilities

Breaker Panel					
Water Heater/Strapping					
Water & Gas Main					
Trash Cans					
Vent Screens/Covers					
Heating/Cooling System					
Other					

5) Garage/Parking

Garage Door/Opener					
Entry Door/Locks					
Floor/Walls/Ceiling					
Lights/Outlets					
Windows					
Other					

6) Laundry

Faucets/Valves					
Plumbing/Drains					
Washer/Dryer					
Other					

B) Interior
1) Entry/Hall

Door/Locks					
Floors/Walls/Ceiling					
Lights/Fan					
Screen Door					
Smoke Detector					
CO2 Detector					
Other					

2) Living Room

Flooring/Baseboards					
Walls/Ceiling					

Windows/Screens					
Lights/Fan					
Switches/Outlets					
Fireplace					
Other					

3) Dining Room

Flooring/Baseboards					
Walls/Ceiling					
Windows/Screens					
Lights/Fan					
Switches/Outlets					
Other					

4) Other/Family/Office

Flooring/Baseboards					
Walls/Ceiling					
Windows/Screens					

Lights/Fan					
Switches/Outlets					
Fireplace					
Other					

5) Kitchen

Flooring/Baseboards					
Windows/Screens					
Lights/Fan					
Switches/Outlets					
Range/Hood					
Oven/Microwave					
Refrigerator					
Dishwasher					
Sink/Disposal					
Faucet/Valves					
Cabinets					

Counters					
Other					
Other					

6) Hall

Flooring/Baseboards					
Walls/Ceiling					
Lights/Switches/Outlets					
Smoke Detector					
CO2 Detector					

7) Bedroom #1

Flooring/Baseboards					
Walls/Ceiling					
Windows/Screens					
Lights/Fan					
Switches/Outlets					
Doors/Locks					

Closet Doors					
Smoke Detector					
Other					

8) Bedroom #2

Flooring/Baseboards					
Walls/Ceiling					
Windows/Screens					
Lights/Fan					
Switches/Outlets					
Doors/Locks					
Closet Doors					
Smoke Detector					
Other					

9) Bedroom #3

Flooring/Baseboards					
Walls/Ceiling					

Windows/Screens					
Lights/Fan					
Switches/Outlets					
Doors/Locks					
Closet Doors					
Smoke Detector					
Other					

10) Bathroom #1

Flooring/Baseboards					
Walls/Ceiling					
Windows/Screens					
Lights/Fan					
Switches/Outlets					
Doors/Locks					
Toilet					
Sink/Faucet					

Tub/Shower					
Shower Door/Curtain					
Towel Racks/TP Holder					
Cabinet/Counters					
Other					

11) Bathroom #2

Flooring/Baseboards					
Walls/Ceiling					
Windows/Screens					
Lights/Fan					
Switches/Outlets					
Doors/Locks					
Toilet					
Sink/Faucet					
Tub/Shower					
Shower Door/Curtain					

Towel Racks/TP Holder					
Cabinet/Counters					
Other					

Notes:

Disclaimer: This report is intended as a visual survey of the property and allows Management to view the physical/cosmetic condition of the property. This survey is not a structural inspection nor do we inspect inaccessible areas. Management shall not be liable for the contents of this report with respect to any structural or inaccessible areas. Any visible problems or preventative maintenance items will be covered in this report, along with our recommendations for repairs, maintenance, or upgrades. Owners who desire a more detailed report are encouraged to contact a licensed property inspection company.

Move out Cleaning Checklist

Kitchen
☐ Work area.
☐ Clean in/outside cupboard doors, remove fingerprints etc. Polish.
☐ Clean cupboard shelves and inside drawers.
☐ Clean cupboard under sink and remove all products.
☐ Clean counters and remove stains.
☐ Clean sink, remove stains, and polish fixtures.
☐ Clean wall around and above sink.

Stove
☐ Clean walls around and above stove.
☐ Clean in/outside hood and fan.
☐ Remove filter, clean; put back.
☐ Clean outside panels and door handle.
☐ Clean control panel.
☐ Clean oven and racks.
☐ Clean storage drawer(s).
☐ Clean broiler pan (if supplied).
☐ Clean stove top and rings.
☐ Clean drip pans or replace them.

Refrigerator
☐ Remove all food. Clean sides, top, door & handles.
☐ Defrost and clean freezer.
☐ Remove and clean shelves and crisper(s).
☐ Clean door shelves and egg tray.
☐ Clean magnetic seal on/around door(s).
☐ Leave refrigerator plugged in and on.
☐ Remember to remove all products from refrigerator.

Dishwasher
☐ Remove items fallen to the bottom.
☐ Remove soap deposit.
☐ Clean along inside of door edges and hinges.
☐ Clean outside door and control panel.

Floors
☐ Wash and wax.

Bathrooms
☐ Clean tub and tub surround, polish fixtures.
☐ Clean sink and soap holder.
☐ Clean in/outside cupboards and drawers.
☐ Clean medicine cabinet, in/out remove personal belongings.
☐ Clean mirror(s).
☐ Clean in/out/around toilet, remove from tank any dye dispenser/tablet, disinfectant.
☐ Wash floor, remove dirt and grime along tub and toilet base.

General Cleaning

☐ Remove all nails from walls (DO NOT FILL OR TOUCH UP PAINT).

☐ Remove marks and fingerprints on walls.

☐ Clean baseboards.

☐ Dust and clean mini blinds.

☐ Clean windowsills, tracks, in/outside glass.

☐ Clean closet shelves and rods.

☐ Remove cobwebs.

☐ Wash all tile/vinyl floors.

☐ Have carpets PROFESSIONALLY cleaned.

Light Fixtures

☐ Dust light fixtures. Remove cover, wash, put back in place.

☐ Clean light bulbs and replace burnt out light bulbs.

☐ Clean switch plates and replace any broken or missing plates.

Fireplace/Wood Stove/Insert

☐ Remove debris and clean.

☐ Clean hearth and mantle.

☐ Clean around wall areas.

Smoke Detector/Alarm(s)

☐ Test alarm(s) and replace batteries if necessary. Retest to insure working order.

Outside

☐ Remove cobwebs from eaves and doorways.

☐ Clean exterior fixtures and replace burnt out bulbs.

☐ Wedge and weed all flowerbeds.

☐ Mow lawn(s).
☐ Remove all debris from grounds and storage area.
☐ Remove all personal belongings from outside.
☐ Broom and clean the garage.
☐ Remove all garbage, recyclable and yard waste containers. Must be left clean if staying with the property.

Repairs
☐ Repair any tenant damage done to the property.
☐ Replace any broken windows.

Last
Please remove all personal belongings. Management will not be responsible for any items left behind. It will be hauled to the dump at tenants' expense. Do a final walkthrough by yourself(s) to double check the list.

ALL ITEMS NOT COMPLETED WILL BE CHARGED TO THE TENANT(S) once keys are turned into office; Security deposit is returned within 21 days (as is required by California law).

Vendor Recommendations:

Tenant Signature: X

Tenant Signature: X

Tenant Signature: X

"Wear and Tear" or "Damages?"

Normal "Wear & Tear" caused by ordinary comings and goings	"Damage" caused by carelessness, abuse,thievery, mysterious disappearance, accident, rules violation, or special request
Well-worn keys	Missing keys
"Sticky" key	Key broken off inside of lock
Difficult door lock	Door lock replaced by tenant without management's permission
De-pressurized fire extinguisher with unbroken seal	De-pressurized fire extinguisher with broken seal (not used to put out fire)
Worn pattern in plastic counter top	Burn in plastic counter top

Rust stain under sink faucet	Sink discolored by clothing or hair dye
Loose, inoperable faucet handle	Missing faucet handle
Discolored ceramic tile	Painted ceramic tile
Loose grout around ceramic tile	Chipped or cracked ceramic tile
Threadbare carpet in hallway	Rust marks on carpet from indoor plant container
Scuffing on wooden floor	Gouge in wooden floor
Linoleum with back showing through	Tear in linoleum
Wobbly toilet	Broken toilet tank lid
Rusty shower curtain rod	Kinked shower curtain rod

Rust stain under bathtub spout	Chip in bathtub enamel
Tracks on door jamb where door rubs	Hole in hollow core door
Door off its hinges and stored in garage	Missing door
Plant hanger left in ceiling	2 inch diameter hole in ceiling
Stain on ceiling caused by leaky roof	Stain on ceiling caused by popping champagne or beer bottles
Cracked paint	Crayon marks on wall
Chipped paint (minor)	Walls painted by tenant in dark color necessitating repainting
Pleasing, professional tenant wallpapering	Amateurish tenant wallpapering

Mildew around shower or tub	Mildew where tenant kept aquarium
Urine odor around toilet	Urine odor in carpet
Discolored light fixture globe	Missing light fixture globe
Odd-wattage light bulbs that work	Burned out or missing light bulbs
Light fixture installed by tenant which fits its location	Light fixture installed by tenant which must be replaced
Window cracked by settling or by high wind	Window cracked by movers
Faded shade	Torn shade
Paint blistered Venetian blinds	Venetian blinds with bent slats
Sun damaged drapes	Pet damaged drapes

Drapery rod which won't close properly	Drapery rod with missing parts
Dirty window screen	Missing bent or torn window screen
Ants inside after rainstorm	Fleas left behind by tenant's pet
Scrawny landscaping which was sparingly watered due to drought conditions	Neglected landscaping which must be replaced with similar plantings
Grease stains on parking space	Caked grease on parking space

Top Ten Legal Mistakes That Can Sink Your Landlord Business

by Attorney Janet Portman

Know the laws in your state before you rent out space.

Being a successful landlord requires lots of practical know-how, business moxie, and familiarity with the market. Until about 30 years ago, the law didn't have much to do with it. Now, however, federal law and most states closely regulate nearly every aspect of your business. Not knowing the rules can land you in lots of legal hot water.

1. Using Generic or Outdated Lease Forms

Most landlords know it's important to have a written lease or rental agreement. But using the wrong form can get you into trouble. So-called "standard" forms that are sold everywhere probably aren't compliant with the laws in your state. If you use a stationery store lease that short-cuts tenants' rights, you could find yourself at the losing end of a lawsuit because of an unenforceable lease clause. On the other hand, some standard forms actually impose greater obligations and restrictions on you than your state's law does! (My favorite requires landlords to return security deposits within ten days, which no state requires.)

2. Asking the Wrong Questions During Applicant Screening

Thorough tenant screening is the most important part of your business – if you choose poorly, you're in for nothing but headaches, with tenants who don't pay the rent, trash your place, or worse. But there are limits to what you can ask. Many landlords don't realize that even well-meaning questions (such as asking a disabled person about his disability or asking if a couple is married) can be illegal forms of discrimination. If the applicant doesn't get the rental, even though your rejection had nothing to do with the offending question, that disappointed tenant has ammunition for a fair housing complaint (which fair housing watch-dog groups are eager to pursue).

3. Setting Policies that Discriminate Against Families

Although it's been illegal to discriminate against families for over 20 years, many owners' practices are far from family-friendly – and are downright illegal. Excluding families because you feel children cause more wear and tear and you prefer a "mature, quiet" environment is illegal. And while you're permitted to limit the number of residents in a unit (in most situations, two occupants per bedroom), you may not apply that standard differently when dealing with families. The cost of this mistake can be another trip to your lawyer's office, to deal with a fair housing complaint.

4. Making Promises That You Don't Deliver On

It's fine to he enthusiastic about the benefits of your property, and it's necessary to do so in competitive markets, but under-stand that your enthusiastic promises will become binding if applicants rely on them when deciding to rent. For example, you may have to deliver the goods if you assure an applicant of a parking space, satellite service or a new paint job. A tenant who feels ripped off may legally break the lease or sue you for the difference in value between what he was promised and what you delivered. Whether the tenant will win is hardly the point – you'll have to respond, which will cost time and money.

5. Charging Excessive Late Fees

Late fees can be a powerful tool to motivate tenants to pay the rent on time. And while a higher fee can be a better motivator, some landlords cross the line, by setting fees that bear little resemblance to the actual damages they suffer when tenants pay late. Courts are increasingly invalidating excessive late fees that can't be justified with hard evidence. You're better off setting a modest fee that reflects your true damages, and dealing with chronic late-payers with pay-or-quit notices.

6. Violating Tenants' Rights to Privacy

Most states have detailed rules on when, for what reasons, and with how much notice you may enter a tenant's home. Yet many landlords stop by unannounced, asking to check things over, perform an on-the-spot repair, or show the place to prospective tenants. Repeated violations of a tenant's privacy (or even one outrageous violation) can excuse a tenant from any further obligations under the lease and may also result in court-ordered money damages against the landlord.

7. Using Security Deposits for the Wrong Projects

The most frequent types of cases heard in small claims court are arguments over security deposit retentions. Yet the basic rule – that deposits should be used only to cover damage beyond wear and tear, needed cleaning, and unpaid rent – isn't hard to understand. Still, landlords routinely use the deposit to cover appliance upgrades, cosmetic improvements and other refurbishing, not repairs. Not surprisingly, many of these landlords lose these cases in small claims court.

8. Ignoring Dangerous Conditions In and Around the Rental

Landlords in virtually every state are required to offer and maintain housing that meets basic health and safety standards, such as those set by state and local building codes, health ordinances, and landlord-tenant laws. If you fail to take care of important repairs, deal with environmental hazards, or respond when your property has become an easy mark for criminals, tenants may break the lease and, in many states, withhold the rent or make the repair themselves and deduct the expense from the rent. Landlords who have failed to make their properties reasonably secure in the face of repeated on-site crime are often ordered to compensate the tenant-victim when yet another criminal intrudes. These are expensive ways to learn the law.

9. Keeping Security Deposits When Tenants Break a Lease

When tenants break a lease and leave early; landlords often keep the entire deposit, reasoning that the tenant 's bad behavior justifies doing so, and that they'll ultimately need it anyway to cover rent. In many states, this is illegal – you must take reasonably prompt steps to re-rent, and credit any new rent toward the tenant's obligation for the rest of the lease. Keeping a two months' rent deposit and re-renting within a month is not legal.

10. Failing to Return Security Deposits According to Law

This list wouldn't be complete without another reference to security deposits. Not only are they used improperly, they' re often not returned according to state law, either. Many states have deadlines by which landlords must itemize their use of the deposit and return any balance. It's not uncommon for tenants to wait many weeks or months for this accounting. In some states, the deliberate or "bad faith" retention of the deposit will result in harsh penalties against the landlord, such as an order that the landlord pay two or three times the deposit to the tenant.

10 Reasons to Hire a Property Manager

By All Property Management Staff

If you've owned income property for any length of time, you know that managing a rental can be financially rewarding. At the same time, you've also likely discovered that property management requires a large commitment of time and effort.

While it may make sense to take the do-it-yourself approach if you're a handy person, live close to your property, and don't mind devoting several hours per month to the task, in many cases this just isn't practical–especially if you hope to expand your business. With this in mind, here are some critical tasks a property manager can help you with:

1. Setting the right rental rates: While looking through the classifieds to see what other landlords are charging for similar properties is a fine way to ballpark your rent price, a good property management company will conduct a thorough market study in order to set a rental price for your property, ensuring that you achieve the perfect balance between maximizing monthly income and maintaining a low vacancy rate.

2. Collecting and depositing monthly rent payments on time: If you've ever worked in a billing department, you know that securing payment from clients can be difficult, not to mention awkward. Property management companies have efficient, tried-and-true systems in place to effectively collect rent and maintain on-time payments. You'll find this particularly important if you have a limited number of properties, and collecting payments on time is crucial to maintaining your cash flow.

3. Marketing and advertising your property: Through long experience, a property manager will know exactly where to market your property and how to craft compelling advertising materials—a significant advantage when it comes to filling your properties quickly and avoiding long vacancies.

4. Finding the right tenants: Experienced property managers are experts at finding good tenants, and will take care of all the details, including the securing all criminal background and security checks, running credit reports, verifying employment, and collecting previous landlord references.

5. Managing tenants: In addition to finding good tenants, a property management company will manage all aspects of the tenant-landlord relationship. The property manager will handle both routine and emergency maintenance, take care of routine inspections, and manage any situations where conflict resolution is required.

6. Managing vendor relationships: Property management companies have relationships with maintenance workers, tradesmen, contractors, suppliers, and vendors that it's almost impossible for an independent landlord to duplicate. Not only will your property manager get you the best work for the best price, they'll oversee any necessary maintenance projects.

7. Ensuring you're compliant with housing regulations & property laws:

There is a multitude of applicable laws and regulations to abide by when renting and maintaining your rental property. These include local, state and federal regulations, as well as fair housing regulations (such as the ADA). A property manager can help you avoid lawsuits by keeping your property up-to-date and in compliance with these regulations.

8. Enabling you to invest in geographically distant properties:
If you manage your own properties, you're pretty much limited to investment opportunities within a tight radius of your own home. By hiring a property manager, you can take advantage of investment deals in any location you wish.

9. Maximizing the profitability of your time:
By having a property manager take care of the day-to-day aspects of running your income property, your free to spend your time identifying further investment opportunities or otherwise furthering your career.

10. Maximizing the profitability of your money:
Most property managers charge a percentage of your property's monthly rental rate in exchange for their services. The rate typically runs anywhere from 6-10%, which is generally less than the money you save by hiring a professional to take care of your property.

Top 10 Things That Get Properties in Trouble In the City of Santa Cruz

1. Parties and loud music.
2. Too many people living there. This leads to many more cars in the neighborhood and parking in front of other people's houses.
3. People living in the garage, living rooms/dens, etc.... converted to bedrooms.
4. Junk, couches, trash, etc.... in the front yard, in the driveway or on the porch.
5. Garbage cans left out on the street after pick-up.
6. Ill-maintained houses. Peeling paint, broken windows, and general dilapidation.
7. Unkempt yards. Weeds, overgrown bushes.
8. Drugs.
9. Late night visitors, loud cars, noise.
10. Working on cars in the driveway for long periods of time.

23 Costly Mistakes Investors Make & How To Avoid Them

By David Lindahl
www.real-estate-fortune.com

1. Waiting too long to start Real Estate investing
2. Not having a plan
3. Not requiring written repair bids every time
4. Not charging tenants for damage
5. Not screening tenants for eviction risk
6. Paying for repair or construction before 100% completion
7. Paying full price for late repair or construction
8. Allowing your real estate business to run your life
9. Over improving your property bought to flip or rent
10. Running out of cash
11. Forgetting about asset protection
12. Over analyzing property (analysis paralysis)
13. Becoming friends with tenants
14. Underinsuring property & risk
15. Ignoring cash flow
16. Punishing bad tenants without rewarding good ones
17. Permitting tenants' problems to spoil the positives of real estate investment
18. Letting rent collections get personal
19. Only looking at properties when there is a problem
20. Missing out on special loan programs

21. Inability to sell a rehab property or to rent a rental property
22. Not thinking of tenants as potential buyers
23. Renting to relatives

www.ingramcontent.com/pod-product-compliance
Lightning Source LLC
Chambersburg PA
CBHW060551200326
41521CB00007B/552